# *My Beautiful Daughter*

# My Beautiful Daughter

*An inspirational true story about a daughters
fight to conquer her drug addiction
through the eyes of her mother.*

Vanessa Wales

authorHOUSE®

*AuthorHouse™*
*1663 Liberty Drive*
*Bloomington, IN 47403*
*www.authorhouse.com*
*Phone: 1-800-839-8640*

*First published by AuthorHouse    12/09/2011*

*ISBN: 978-1-4678-8716-8 (sc)*
*ISBN: 978-1-4678-8715-1 (ebk)*

*Printed in the United States of America*

*Any people depicted in stock imagery provided by Thinkstock are models, and such images are being used for illustrative purposes only. Certain stock imagery © Thinkstock.*

*This book is printed on acid-free paper.*

*Because of the dynamic nature of the Internet, any web addresses or links contained in this book may have changed since publication and may no longer be valid. The views expressed in this work are solely those of the author and do not necessarily reflect the views of the publisher, and the publisher hereby disclaims any responsibility for them.*

# *Dedication*

I have dedicated this book to the memory of my father Frederick Gomer whose courage and unconditional love for his family inspired me to write.

# Acknowledgements

I have so many people to thank.

To Richard for being my rock, whilst putting up with my insanity and tunnel vision.

Rachel for having the courage to help all the family whilst coping with her own heartache.

Jane for taking the time to give love and support to me and her family.

Mathew my son and my joy who battled with his feelings and won.

Joan my mother a constant support.

To my friends and neighbours Barbara, Jane, Heather and Richard.

My heartfelt thanks for always being there for us and helping whenever you could.

To Sue a treasured friend.

To Mike and Bobbi my thanks for being the best employers and friends that I could wish for, never judging only supporting.

For Gerry a shoulder for Richard.

And Shirley the voice of reason.

I thank all the doctors, nurses, key workers and counsellors that looked after my daughter and helped cure her of her addiction and health problems.

To my sister Julie I am grateful for your advice and loyalty.

To my Publishers for helping a novice writer to get her little book printed and her message across.

And finally my Beautiful Daughter and her partner for allowing this book to be written.

I am so proud of you.

An hour passed and I was just going to bed when I heard a loud sobbing on the landing. I thought this was just another tantrum, and went upstairs to see what Louise was doing, and to my horror the scene that unfolded to me was Louise standing on the landing holding my gift wrapped birthday present, crying with blood pouring from her wrists, and shouting "I am so sorry Mum."

"What on earth have you done?" I screamed and just managed to get her back into the bedroom. By this time James and Ryan had come upstairs only to witness the bloody scene in the bedroom. I wiped her wounds, and saw that she had been self harming, and although she had cut herself in several places, had luckily avoided her main arteries. "Mum" she whimpered "Don't hate me."

Hate her, what kind of a statement was that? I could never hate her, I loved her, "Lou what is it?" I asked, "Why are you doing this?" I was scared of the answer as I didn't know what the answer would be. Her father and brother stood in the doorway stunned and confused. "Mum I am going to tell you something." She mumbled through the tears, "I have been taking drugs." "What drugs" I asked, expecting her to say ecstasy, or dope or something like that. "Heroin!" she gasped. My heart seemed to surge, the words couldn't seem to come.

James and Ryan stood for what seemed to be an age everything seemed to go into slow motion, "Mum I'm sorry so sorry." Louise was now shaking and in that instant I knew we were not hearing lies, this was reality, our darling daughter was taking heroin, the one thing that all parents dread had happened to Louise, she was taking heroin.

# Chapter 1

## IN THE BEGINNING

*A*s I drove into the car park of the college I was excited but a little apprehensive. The building was very formidable and there were hundreds of people wandering around and entering the great hall. After battling to park my car without having to reverse into a space, as this is not my strongest skill, I followed the ensuing crowd into the building and made my way to a table in the corner, trying to be inconspicuous, and sat alone watching the hustle and bustle around me.

As I observed the shuffling of seats and general mumblings from the crowd, my mind wandered back twenty three years,

I found myself thinking about how the events of the past years had changed the way I thought about life and the challenges it brought on a daily basis.

Everyone in the hall probably had a story to tell, but how many had experienced what I considered the devastation of drug addiction I wondered.

As the noise from the crowd dimmed into the background I thought back to the time that my life changed from hair salon owner to becoming a new Mum again.

It was nineteen eighty seven and we were in the era of big hair, and leg warmers, lycra footless tights, baggy tops and high waisted jeans.

On Top of the pops was George Benson, and in between selling my hairdressing business, and getting re-married, I was about to give birth to my third child.

From a previously unhappy marriage, I had managed to produce two lovely girls now aged seventeen and fourteen.

Emma being the eldest had just started work, and was enjoying a bit of freedom with her friends.

She was commuting to London every day working in a jewellers, and although at first had found the travelling a bit daunting, was looking forward to passing her driving test and having her first car.

Holly on the other hand was in the throes of thinking she was misunderstood by me, and being a teenager, she had found it difficult to change schools and make new friends, as we had moved to a different area.

Both my daughters had been affected in different ways by the divorce of my first husband, and understandably were very suspicious of Ryan when he first entered their lives.

Emma being the eldest had witnessed first-hand the obvious animosity between her father and myself, but had never really got on with him as they clashed on many occasions, so was glad when the marriage was over. Holly though, being younger, had not experienced the same, therefore missed her father and was angry for a while about the break up.

I had met and fallen in love with Ryan after my divorce eighteen months before. He had come into my salon to have a haircut and we seemed to click almost immediately. For some unknown reason not only was I attracted to him, but I had a strange feeling that he would be part of my life, so I was over the moon when he asked me out to dinner. We became inseparable and he set about slowly starting to get to know the girls, never pushing himself on them as he was not that sort of person and he wanted them to feel happy and comfortable in his company, and this he felt had to come naturally.

My parents had met him and had taken an instant liking to him.

After a few months he popped the question, and I accepted, although we needed to see if

Emma and Holly were ok about it as they had been through so much upheaval and I wanted them to be happy to. I was nervous as we sat them down to ask if they would be happy if we got married and became a family.

They were not surprised at our question as they knew we were in love.

Both said it was great and there were hugs all round.

My phone became very hot as I rang everyone on the planet to give the good news. It was wonderful that my parents were so pleased that I had found a new partner that would look after me and the girls, and Dad especially looked forward to giving me away, while Mum started organising the event.

At last we were married and I discovered I was pregnant.

We were overjoyed and couldn't wait to tell everyone, but we had to tell the girls first. Both Ryan and I were nervous as we had no idea what the reaction might be. Again we sat them down and told them of our news, expecting them to be a bit taken back, but this time they did not seem to be happy at all, Emma was silent and Holly started to cry. We did not understand why, as we assumed they would have been pleased. Ryan and I looked at each other both a bit stunned at the reaction, so he left me to have a private conversation with them to get to the bottom of it.

It turned out that they both thought they would not be loved as much as the new arrival, as they were not Ryan's children, and felt as though they were going to be pushed aside. I was so upset that they would think that, as they meant everything to me, so I turned to Emma and said. "When I had Holly, I did not stop loving you, so why would I stop loving both of you by having another child?" They sat for a moment and realised what I had just said, and both looked relieved. With that explained we all celebrated by going out to dinner as a family. After a shaky start, both of my daughters were getting used to their new life with my husband Ryan, and were looking forward to having either a new brother or sister.

We had moved to a flat on the Isle of Dogs and we were all settling in to our new surroundings. Ryan was thrilled at the prospect of having his first child.

Having already taken on two teenage girls, he now had a great insight to what being a good dad involved, and he was up for the challenge. I had realised early on in our relationship that he was going to be a wonderful father as he was proving that already, with the love and support he had shown to my other children.

He was very patient when being challenged by my daughters about what times to be home, or keeping their rooms tidy, all the normal clashes that occur when a new a family is getting to know each other. Through all this I was confident that they were happy, as I was watching my girls beginning to accept him as their new male role model.

Ryan conscious of his new role of provider, had been training to be a financial advisor. This took a lot of study and hard work but he managed to pass all his exams with distinctions, enabling him to start working self-employed as an independent pension specialist. Emma in the meantime passed her driving test and Ryan put money towards buying her first car. She was thrilled at the prospect of being able to be more independent and I was happy seeing her blossom into such a beautiful woman.

Well the day finally came, my waters had broken in the early hours of the morning and Ryan was trying to be cool and calm while phoning the hospital.

I was more concerned that I was standing in the lounge not knowing what to put on or how to stop the continue flow of the water.

The fact that it was Friday the 13th didn't worry me; I was convinced that this was my lucky day.

I had decided that being the third time in labour, I would be cool calm and collected. I was determined to enjoy the experience with full makeup and wearing a pretty nightie.

I woke up Holly and Emma, and informed them that we were leaving.

Needless to say both girls were less than excited at being disturbed so early in the morning, and we left with some strange grunts of "Ok then!" coming from the bedrooms.

Everything was going to plan as I lay in splendour in the private room, sipping fruit juice and being told by my midwife how good I was being and that I was near to delivery. The mood in the room was calm, Ryan held my hand and I felt safe. After a 12 hour labour my Louise made her first appearance, weighing in at 8 pounds 11 ounces. I looked at her and immediately had the same wonderful feeling of love for her as I did with my other babies.

Ryan had been with me all through the labour, popping out for a bite to eat on my insistence, just managing to get back just in time to see his daughter arrive.

He knew he had to hurry up the corridor as he heard a lot of noise coming from my room. As he entered the bay, I was in throws of giving birth with full makeup smeared all over the bed sheets and white knuckles holding on to the gas and air. If he had come within one inch of the gas mask he would have been in serious trouble. My idea of a calm serene enjoyable birth was long forgotten I just wanted my baby to be born. Then all at once it was over. Louise gave a cry and I was hooked, and memories of the pain disappeared in an instance.

As I looked at Ryan I saw the same look in his eyes too, he was so proud and excited and couldn't wait to hold her close. "Does Dad want to hold his daughter?" enquired the midwife. Before she got an answer Ryan held out his hands and Louise was placed in his arms. Both Ryan and I stared at this little angel for what seemed an age, whilst the midwife was sorting me out at the other end. My dignity had gone out the window but all I could think about was how wonderful this tiny baby was.

She was so beautiful, she had a hint of blond hair and her skin was so clear and pink, she had little chubby cheeks and cupid bow lips.

Her eyes were wide open looking at the world she had entered. "She's perfect" whispered Ryan. Yes as far as we were concerned she was the most perfect baby in the world. I was so happy and contented knowing that my family was complete and that Louise and my other daughters were in safe hands with Ryan.

We took her home and the girls welcomed their new sibling, and in between being teenagers, helped with the care of little Louise.

Over the next few days there were many comings and goings, as Louise was introduced to all the family.

My parents were overjoyed for us and Mum fell in love with our little bundle at once.

Ryan's father had passed away six months before, so it had been a bitter sweet moment for his mother when she came to see her grandchild for the first time, as she missed her husband and was still grieving over her loss.

We were not able to see her very much as she lived six hours away, so it was lovely that she managed to come for a visit. Ryan conscious of this and being a very proud father, delighted in showing her off to his mother.

After a few months I became pregnant again and this time we had a boy.

As before, Ryan was with me, and witnessed the birth of James.

This time it had been a difficult birth and he arrived battered and bruised, but just as lovely, and although his blonde hair and big ice blue eyes were overshadowed by his scrunched up face and crumpled ears, he blossomed very quickly and became real little charmer. We bought him home and he joined the family with Louise, who was now fourteen months old.

She had been a perfect baby, sleeping well at night, happy and contented, and now was just beginning to walk. James on the other hand refused to sleep, did not take kindly to the bottle and was generally a bad tempered baby when not in my arms.

The years rolled by and Louise started school, she had always been a quiet child very well behaved and polite. We could take her anywhere and she would always set a good example to her brother. James however was prone to acting up on occasion, but he was a lovable rogue so got away with it most of the time.

James craved attention always getting it with his infectious laughter that would fill a room. Louise on the other hand would sit quietly, happy to just play with her toys, never demanding anything.

As both progressed through school Louise excelled but James struggled, and at the age of seven was diagnosed with dyslexia and dyspraxia.

I was informed by the local dyslexia centre that most prisoners were dyslexic, and that he would not achieve any qualifications unless he had one to one teaching. I was unable to get extra help for him at school unless he went through a long process of tests. I learnt that even if James was diagnosed officially with dyslexia, he would not automatically be entitled to receive one to one teaching, and that to get statemented could take months.

This was unacceptable to both Ryan and I, as we felt it was precious time wasted.

We decided that I would take a course to learn how to support our son and help James at home with his reading as we were determined that he would have every opportunity to reach his full potential.

I also had to make sure he did his exercises for his dyspraxia.

This condition I had been told had been partially caused by the fact that James had not crawled as a baby, but had decided to stand at six months.

We were unaware of this and considered him to be very advanced for his age, but we later had learnt that there is a good reason for crawling, as it allows the small motor muscles that help with writing and balance to develop properly, and as James had always complained of aching fingers when he wrote and got tired very easily when using a pen, it made sense to me.

We were given a strict regime of exercises to help with this and James was thrilled at the prospect of all the attention he was going to get.

We were always careful to include Louise in his activities as we were concerned that she wouldn't feel left out in any way, but most of the time she sat in the room quietly watching the events. I later wondered whether I had unintentionally ignored her because of this, and so she had become a little isolated, whilst my attentions were taken up by her ever energetic brother.

As they grew older we became aware of the drug problems that were emerging on our doorstep, so decided that we would move away in the hope that we could shield our precious children from that threat.

A friend of mine had first knowledge of this problem through her son's addiction, and knowing how devastating that had been for her family, we felt it would be better to move to the country.

After much searching we found what we considered to be the perfect place, a sleepy village in the heart of Devon. My parents had moved there a few months earlier, and so we were excited at the prospect of a gentle village life. As my eldest daughter Emma lived in Kent with her partner and young son, I felt that it would be nice that they would have a place to come on holiday, and we would only be three hours away.

We told Emma of our intentions and she was more than happy for us, and I looked forward to having my young grandson stay for holidays when he was older. Although Emma lived a short distance from us we only seemed to have time to see each other occasionally, although we spoke on the phone a lot.

Her time was taken up with the everyday hard work of bringing up her son Alex and running a home. Alex was a sweet child but had Attention Deficit Hyperactive Disorder, so could be very demanding at times but Emma coped magnificently with his problems.

Our other daughter Holly was single and working abroad.

She had just left a dysfunctional relationship and felt the need to leave the country and try something new.

We moved in the autumn and as Ryan's career meant that he could work on the internet as well as travelling to see his clients, it seemed we had made the right decision. The local schools were small and very family orientated, so I knew the children would settle in quickly and make new friends.

For a while life seemed ideal, little did we know what was in store for us, and how it would impact on all of us individually.

# *Chapter 2*

## THE CHANGE

Our Lou, as we sometimes called her, was 14 years old, and she was growing into a loving beautiful girl, with so much to look forward to.

She had kept her blonde hair which was now half way down her back, and was becoming very particular over what she was wearing. We were glad we had an en-suite as she was spending more and more time in the bathroom, much to James's disgust, as he was only in there for two minutes at the most, he was at the age where boys seem to become allergic to washing.

She had also started going round with a girl from school. Her name was Samantha, but she liked to be called Sammi. Her hair was dyed dark brown with light brown roots and she wore pale makeup with thick mascara. Ryan said she looked like a panda, and was not very impressed.

We were not keen on her as she was very loud and a bit too bubbly for our taste but then we thought that Louise, being very quiet, would probably benefit from her friendship and begin to come out of her shell by mixing with her.

Also being mindful that she was growing up, we allowed her to go to the local disco once a week and have sleep over's with her friend, that was what everyone seemed to do at that time.

I had met her friend's parents and they seemed very sensible and we took it in turns to take the girls to the disco each weekend and pick them up, so no harm would come to them. This was all suddenly to change one weekend, although we did not realise it at the time. Louise went to stay with her friend and was going to the local disco as usual. We assumed that Sammi's parents would be taking them to and from their home as we always did it when it was our turn.

So we bade her farewell and looked forward to seeing her when she came home on the Sunday.

Louise was home earlier than normal on Sunday so we assumed that Sammi had other arrangements and so we did not think any more about it.

When she came in nothing seemed unusual, although she may have been a little quieter than normal, and not willing to talk about her night at the disco.

I thought this was strange as she would normally be gushing about the evening and driving us mad telling us about all the fun she had while staying over her friend's house.

Like most teenagers she thought her friends parents were much more exciting than the dull lifestyle she considered we led. I felt that I was being a hip Mum to respect her wishes and did not ask her any more questions. I told her to make sure her homework was up to date, and she went upstairs and stayed there, even having her tea in her room, until she got up the next day for school.

Louise left for school the next morning not waiting for James as she usually did and I did not blame her, as I was too busy trying to get James to emerge from his room and wash before leaving for school he could be hard work sometimes.

Ryan and I noticed that when the next weekend arrived, Lou was not keen to go out and for the first time in ages she stayed home, spending most of her time in her room doing her homework and playing with the cat.

Over the next few weeks Louise seemed to develop a bit of an attitude problem, we put it down to teenage angsed, so joked about it saying that if attitude was all we got then we were lucky.

We had also been more preoccupied with the return of Holly from working abroad; she had met a new man and they had moved in together and rented a house in the next village.

We were introduced to him one evening at a family get together.

His name was Paul, and we all spent the evening getting to know him.

Holly looked very happy and laughed at all his jokes.

Ryan bonded with him straight away, as Paul laughed at all Ryan's jokes.

I was pleased as he seemed to fit in, and obviously adored Holly.

Emma had also relocated to our area as her relationship had broken down and now having two children, she wanted to be nearer us and we were very happy that she had made that decision as I could now see more of Alex and his baby brother Timmy.

After a while we noticed that although Louise was going out, her friend Sammi did not call and Lou was not in any mood to talk about it so we assumed they had probably had a falling out and so we left her to sort that out for herself.

Then she decided to not be bothered to do her homework, wanted to go out all the time, was not adhering to home rules, had no remorse when told off about her attitude, and seemed to purposely try and upset the household.

James was also being affected by her attitude as she had started to bully him a little at school, by pushing him around when they were in the playground.

This had upset him so much that he came home one day and burst into tears.

When I confronted her she said she was only joking and that he was making a fuss. I knew that James was telling the truth as he was not one to cry easily, so decided that it would stop it immediately, as I would not tolerate behaviour of that sort from any of my children and warned her not to do it again.

When I told Ryan he put it down to teenage behaviour and took her to one side explaining that her attitude would have to change and she needed to leave her brother alone.

My sister was living in Greece and we were going to visit her with Mum and Dad, Louise and James.

Louise had announced she had a boyfriend and although we hadn't met him, or knew anything about him, she seemed to need to see him every day or it was the end of the world.

This was obviously why she had not been seeing Sammi at the weekends anymore, we thought.

Needless to say Louise did not want to come away with us, but we insisted and thought it would be an ideal way of spending quality time with us in a relaxed environment.

James had also become more distant to her and we suspected they were still not getting on, so we hoped that this would also help to build bridges between them.

Louise now fifteen made sure we understood that she didn't want to be with us and was an absolute nightmare all the time we were away.

She did this by refusing to walk with us, not eating with us, not taking part in swimming or any activities, and generally being a right pain.

We also never knew where she was, as she would wander off around the holiday park and on her own for hours.

When we visited my sister, she sat in sullen silence most of the time and made us feel very uncomfortable.

My parents tried to act as though nothing was happening, but Ryan and I were seething and couldn't wait to get her home to give her a good telling off.

We arrived back and Louise immediately wanted to see her boyfriend, we said no, but we then had a big tantrum, and by now both Ryan and I were so exhausted with it all we let her go for some peace.

This was not the way that we would normally have dealt with the situation, but we were so tired of her behaviour we just wanted time to work out how best to stop this continual battle and get our daughter to stop fighting us.

Over the next few weeks things continued to get worse, she had now left school and had got a job in the financial world, we thought that things would be better now as she was growing up and would stop this behaviour.

How naive were we?

We finally met the boyfriend and almost immediately decided that he wasn't good enough.

He was a bit arrogant and had the same sort of manner as Louise, and she seemed to cling on to his every word, so we decided that it was him that had influenced our daughter to act like this and therefore he was to blame.

Ryan and I decided to wait it out until she grew tired of him as we were both convinced she would see sense then would realise how silly she had been and get rid of him.

We began to notice that Louise seemed to be drinking a bit too much and a couple of times acted slightly drunk.

Ryan pulled her up on this on many occasions with no success so we hoped that her hangovers would put her off and that she would learn by her own mistakes.

We tried to sit her down on many occasions to talk to her, and ask if she had any problems, she would always deny that she had any and didn't seem to want to talk about it.

My birthday was in December and we were all looking forward to Christmas.

Louise was becoming more and more distant, and try as we may; she was not willing to talk to either her us or her older sisters.

James had become fed up with her constant bickering and selfishness so hardly spoke to her.

A few days before my birthday Louise was in late, as usual, and I had just about come to the end of my patience and as soon as she walked into the door I let her have it. I told her a few home truths, and demanded an explanation to why she had once again felt it was all right to disregard us and come home when she pleased. Louise needed to understand what it was doing to her as well as us.

We were constantly worried about her safety as the boyfriend left her to make her own way home every night.

We had the usual stomping up the stairs and slamming of doors, but this time I followed her in and shouted at her, telling her that she would have to leave home if she didn't stop this behaviour, not meaning a word of it but I just felt I had to try and shock her into realising that we were not her enemy.

I was near to tears and Ryan having heard the commotion came up the stairs to see what the matter was. When he saw how upset I was he also went in the bedroom and read her the riot act.

Ryan usually left the discipline to me as he did not want to come across as the bad cop. He had not had the close relationship that he would have liked with his own father as he felt he was sometimes too strict so this had caused distance between them. The last thing Ryan wanted was the same thing to happen with his children and would only intervene when I needed support, but on this occasion having had enough of her uncaring cavalier attitude he needed to have his say. Louise was clearly shaken by her father's words but said nothing and I could see her eyes filling up as he left her to think about things.

An hour passed and I was just going to bed when I heard loud sobbing on the landing. I thought this was just another tantrum, and went upstairs to see what Louise was doing, and to my horror the scene that unfolded to me was Louise standing on the landing holding my gift wrapped birthday present, crying with blood pouring from her wrists, and shouting "I am so sorry Mum."

"What on earth have you done?" I screamed. and just managed to get her back into the bedroom.

By this time James and Ryan had come upstairs only to witness the bloody scene in the bedroom.

I wiped her wounds, and saw that she had been self-harming, and although she had cut herself in several places, had luckily avoided her main arteries.

"Mum" she whimpered "Don't hate me."

Hate her, what kind of a statement was that? I could never hate her, I loved her.

"Lou what is it?" I asked.

"Why are you doing this?" I was scared of the answer as I didn't know what the answer would be.

Her father and brother stood in the doorway stunned and confused.

"Mum I am going to tell you something." She mumbled through the tears, "I have been taking drugs."

"What drugs" I asked, expecting her to say ecstasy, or dope or something like that.

"Heroin!" she gasped.

My heart seemed to surge, the words just couldn't seem to come.

James and Ryan stood for what seemed to be and age everything seemed to go into slow motion, "Mum I'm sorry so sorry."

Louise was now shaking and in that instant I knew we were not hearing lies, this was reality; our darling daughter was taking heroin, the one thing that all parents dread had happened to Louise, she was taking heroin. The words went round and round in my head, suddenly I had the uncontrollable urge to hit her but cuddle her too. I chose to take her in my arms and hold her so tight, saying it will be all right we will get this sorted out.

We were all in tears; James was distraught, as were Ryan and I.

We sat there just holding on to her trying to understand why this was happening to us, how did this happen? we were a decent family, loving and supportive of our children, this could not happen to us.

Unfortunately it can enter anyone's life, drug addiction does not discriminate class creed or gender, it is the nature of the beast, and this is how I would come to view it. "How long have you been doing this?" I asked. "Since I was fourteen," she replied. This was another blow, were we so out of touch with our daughter? I had just been told my beautiful daughter had been taking drugs for two years and we didn't know, what kind of parents were we to have not noticed any symptoms?

What had made her start taking drugs? I was convinced it must have been her boyfriend, as I could not blame her.

"Does the boyfriend take drugs too?" I asked

"Only dope" she said. We didn't believe her but this was not the time for blame we had to get our daughter well, but how could we do that? where would we go? Ryan by now had plucked his daughter from the bed and was holding on to her telling her that he would do everything possible to help her through this. James just seemed to stand in the doorway stunned and shaking.

Louise by now was sobbing and trembling in her father's arms not daring to let go and Ryan and I looked at each other in disbelief and fear.

This was only the beginning, and we all knew it would be a long journey.

# *Chapter 3*

## COMING TO TERMS WITH THE NEWS

The night we found out that Louise was taking heroin was probably the worst night that we had spent since her birth. The same words were going round and round in my head, my child is a heroin addict, she is going to die, what are we going to do? Every time I looked at her I saw the sweet five year old that played for hours with her Barbie dolls house, and with her cat ginger.

How she loved her cat, he even allowed her to dress him up in her dolls clothes, and wheel him around the garden in her pushchair.

She had always been very good with animals she had a real rapport with them, so much so that at an early age had decided to be a vet.

In her last year at school Louise applied and was accepted to go to college to become a veterinary nurse. This was the only thing she wanted to do and, until she met her boyfriend, she was making arrangements to live in, and come home at weekends. Suddenly, out of the blue, she had decided that it was not for her and opted for a job in a bank.

We were surprised and worried that she had so suddenly changed her mind, but once again put it down to her not being able to see her boyfriend during the week. Although we tried to understand, she seemed to need to see him every day, this we felt was unhealthy, and blamed him thinking he must be controlling her. After the revelations the night before Ryan and I got up, ready to talk to Lou about how we would be able to get the help she needed. Louise had already got up early to go to work, and I just caught her as she was leaving home.

It was 7am, too early for the bus but she said she was getting a lift and that she was going to see the doctor that evening to arrange a detox, and she would see us that evening.

My mind must have been in such turmoil that I did not question why she was getting a lift so early in the morning, when she was seeing the doctor after work.

"Lou, I can come with you if you like." I said.

"No Mum I need to do this myself," she quickly replied, and with that she was gone, leaving me in total shock.

Ryan and I had no idea what to do or where to go.

We had spent most of the night going over what had been revealed, and trying to make some sort of sense of it.

If she had been taking drugs for so long how could we have not noticed?

As we mulled over the events of the past two years things began to click.

We remembered wondering why her pupils sometimes seemed to be like pin pricks, and other times like saucers. Lou had always been well proportioned, but of late had lost weight; I had put this down to dieting, as she had become fussy with her food. Her appearance had deteriorated, and her clothes seemed to smell dank. We had become used to her mood swings, and after one of her many rants she did not seem to show any emotion she just carried on as if nothing had happened. We were beginning to be unable to recognise the girl that lived with us, as we only occasionally saw glimpses of the daughter we knew and loved.

The first thing we felt we had to do was inform her sisters.

I was going to deal with this as Ryan had to go to work and needed to have his mind focused on that as he had to travel a long way and I didn't want him to have any more worries at the moment. I made arrangements to see her eldest sister first. Emma had for a long time been upset at Louise's behaviour not understanding how we were able to cope with the continual mood swings and tantrums.

Having young children of her own, one of which was getting more difficult as he got older, she was dreading them becoming teenagers and did not know if she would be able to cope. She had on many occasions apologised for the way she behaved when she was in her teens. It's something we all go through and its hoped that your children will come out the other end unscathed, parents on the other hand pray that they will survive too.

Emma knew as soon as she saw my face that I had some bad news, this was going to be so hard as I was not sure if I could actually say the words without sobbing, but I was determined to try and stay focussed. We sat down and as calmly as I could, told her of the revelations that had unfolded the night before.

She sat in silence, her eyes welling up with tears, and as I mentioned the word heroin she gave a loud gasp and the tears flowed. Then her expression changed and became that of disbelief and shock.

Emma had so many questions she wanted to be answered, but there were no reasonable answers that I could think of. Emma being the eldest of my children was very protective of me as we had been through so much in the past, but this was beyond any understanding and she was concerned how it was affecting me.

So we hugged trying to convince each other that everything was going to be ok, and that this would just be a blip.

"I will come with you to see Holly Mum." She said after wiping her now puffy eyes. I was pleased that she would be there as Holly was very close to Lou.

Both Emma and I approached the door and Holly opened it and immediately knew that we were not just visiting but there was a good reason we were there together. We broke the news to her as best we could, and she was just as devastated as we all were, so we sat together for most of the day in tears.

They both wanted to hug her but at the same time were very angry with her.

The only way I can describe the feelings we were experiencing was bereavement, we were mourning the loss of our daughter and sister who had become someone that we didn't know. They could not understand why she had done this and that it was not just the occasional pills or dope but heroin a serious habit forming, life changing, hard drug. How could this be happening to Louise? She was such a dear sweet girl but had begun to turn into an unfeeling stranger. We all agreed, it must be the boyfriend that was to blame, and we wished him gone from her life. Exhausted with it all I left them together, as it was clear that they both needed time as we all did, to come to terms with the news, but we would all be there for Louise come what may.

When I arrived home Ryan was in the kitchen, staring into an empty glass, looking lost and worried. He had come home early from work unable to function, his mind in turmoil. As I sat down he looked up and the tears were flowing, he couldn't speak, he just sat there and wept. I had never seen him like this before, it was sinking in that his precious daughter was going to have to fight to get her life back, and both he and I blamed ourselves for her predicament as we had to ultimately have done something wrong for her to be so far into an addiction without us knowing. Ryan and I just sat in silence, not knowing what was in store for us, and praying that she would come through this.

That evening Louise did not come home after work, or call, we assumed she had gone round to her boyfriends and called him.

She was there and said she would be home on the last bus.

"How did you get on at the doctors?" I asked

"Ok" she answered, "I will talk to you when I get home."

And with that she said goodbye and hung up.

To say that I was beginning to lose patience was an understatement, we had just been told that she was on drugs but we were still being treated with the same distance and disrespect that was becoming the norm.

I waited up for her to find out what was going to happen and when she finally arrived she seemed to just want to ignore my questions, but this time I was determined to have my say. As she moved towards the stairs to get to her room I blocked her way. Lou knew this time there would be no escape.

Once again I asked how she got on at the doctors.

"I have decided to have a home detox Mum," she said.

"The nurse says that it would be the best for me and they have had good results from this method."

"What will it entail and how will I be able to help you?" I asked

"You will administer the drugs and keep an eye on me, the nurse will visit every day for two weeks and the drug social worker will also be round to advise and council me." she quickly replied.

"As I am a young drug user I come under a different department to adult services." She ended.

Lou seemed quite positive, and for that moment I felt that the end was near and that I would have my daughter back fit and healthy again.

Then I asked a question that had been baffling me. My daughter from an early age had always fainted at the sight of a needle. She had to lie down when she was young when she had her immunisation jabs, as she would collapse, so how could she possibly be doing this to herself, I still felt she must be making a mistake and was popping pills not injecting heroin, how silly of me, but I suppose rational thoughts were not going through my head at the time.

"I don't inject Mum I smoke it," was the reply. Well that was an answer I didn't expect. I didn't even know that you could smoke heroin, then I thought, well it can't be so bad if she is smoking it,

"So you will be weaned of it completely then in two weeks Louise?" I enquired hopefully.

"Oh yes but I must go to bed now as I have a busy day tomorrow and the nurse is coming next week to start the detox."

As I watched her disappear upstairs, I began to feel that it was going to be ok, and that I would be able to look after her and the nurse and social worker would fill me in on what to expect and how to come to terms with this terrible situation.

I was not even thinking about the fact that Lou was slightly slurring her words, and that her right eye seemed to blink out of sync with the left, I just felt relieved that treatment would start soon and that this nightmare would soon be over. Ryan had not been able to go to sleep and I filled him in on the details.

He, like me was hopeful, and relieved that I was willing cope at home with the treatment as he had so many work commitments to carry out, it would have been impossible for him to take the time off to help. I would also have the extra support from the girls, while James kept his distance.

# *Chapter 4*

## THE FIGHT BEGINS

*J* had been working part time in a residential home as an activities organiser, and needed to be very positive with my clients. This was going to be very difficult as forward planning and total commitment was essential. I had thought about it for a couple of days and after talking it over with Ryan, had decided that Louise needed me to be there for her and she came first, so I had no choice but to hand in my notice. I was dreading this as it would mean that I would have to explain the reasons why, and didn't know what excuse to give, as I really could not see myself uttering the words that had destroyed our world.

As usual, all the staff had greeted me as I arrived with the usual smiles and jokes but today I was in no frame of mind to be the jolly person that I had to portray. Moving past the staff room I entered the lounge only to be confronted by Hilda, one of the residents, she grabbed my arm and with a concerned look said,

"I don't like that colour on you it's too dark"

As we looked at each other for a moment I smiled to myself, as she was standing beside me wearing a pink dress with an orange cardigan and for some reason only known to her, sporting a large blue hat.

I was wearing black, an unconscious decision on my part but it must have echoed the way I was feeling.

"Thank you for your advice Hilda" I answered.

"That is all right dear I will knit you a yellow scarf so you will be brighter."

With that announcement Hilda made her way to the stock cupboard and pulled out some yellow and purple wool and after negotiating round the other residents, found her favourite chair and began the task of brightening me up.

As I continued through the dining room I entered the lounge where other residents had seated themselves in anticipation of my arrival. They greeted me with smiles and the odd walking stick was waved in the air. They knew that when I arrived there would be some sort of entertainment to brighten up a normally dull day.

"What have we got today?" A familiar voice asked.

It was Jesse, my favourite, she was a one of ladies that enjoyed making cards when we had our art afternoon. I turned and looked at their eager faces, but this afternoon would be different and I felt sad to let them down.

"Not sure yet Jesse!" I replied, as I carried on making my way through the lounge.

As I proceeded on up the stairs, avoiding the chair lift, to the main office I was rehearsing my excuses determined to be calm.

I stood outside for a moment to try and compose myself, took a deep breath, knocked on the door and entered the small room.

"Can I have a quick word with you Marion?" I whispered.

Marion was the manager and had been the one to that had interviewed me.

I had a good working relationship with her and the owners of the home, so felt I could tell them my daughter was unwell and they would be understanding.

As she turned to look at me I suddenly lost control, my well-rehearsed speech was forgotten and I immediately burst into uncontrollable tears.

"Oh my God whatever is the matter?" she asked.

How I managed to speak is still a mystery to me but suddenly I seemed to blurt out, "my daughter is very ill and I must leave to look after her".

"Of course you must," she replied.

By this time she was beginning to fill up too.

"May I ask what is wrong with her?" she gently enquired.

Well in between sobbing I managed to tell her my awful news.

"We have just found out Lou is a heroin addict and I have to detox her at home." My speech was almost illegible as my voice just seemed to come and go between sobbing.

As the words faded there was a long pause that seemed to last for ages, then suddenly in that instance she put her hand on mine and did what we all seem to do when another person is in pain, she gently patted my hand.

It's as if a pat or a touch will heal all ills and it was at that moment realised I was not alone.

As I sat in the office telling her everything that had occurred, she was in tears too, still holding on to my hand.

I later discovered that she had been through the same thing with a family member and after many years it was still happening.

My employers were informed and after giving me a hug, with the mandatory patting on the back, I was released immediately to do what had to be done.

Luckily the staff at the home were able to do a quiz that afternoon so the residents had some kind of activity, and I crept out of the home, via the back door, not knowing if I would ever return.

I arrived home red eyed and again exhausted from it all, and the fight had hardly begun. Was I going to be able to do this? I wondered I don't mind admitting that I was very frightened, as I had no idea what to expect.

The day finally arrived and I had spent most of my time keeping busy getting the housework up to date as I wanted to concentrate on giving my daughter all my attention for the next couple of weeks, and making sure she would have every comfort in her room.

Ryan left for work early that morning and as he left, kissed me and squeezed my hand. "Good luck with today I will be thinking of you," he said as he gave me another kiss. As he walked out the door I thought this was the day that we will start to get Lou well.

Louise had managed to get time off from work as a holiday so that no-one would know what she was about to embark on.

The nurse arrived mid-morning, and I greeted her with a coffee and sat down ready to be given the information that was needed.

Louise was upstairs getting dressed so this gave me ample time to ask the nurse about the treatment and what my role in all this would be.

The nurse explained to me that Louise would have a physical examination and in order to give her the right dose of the cocktail of drugs to detox her, she would have to talk to her about the amount and type of drugs she had been using.

Then if she was happy with her state of mind and general health Louise would be given all her medication and I would have to administer it.

I was told that the after effects were different with each individual, so to expect a number of different symptoms including, cold sweats, shaking, mood swings, sickness, diarrhoea, low blood pressure, weakness, and general flu symptoms.

"Is there anything that I should look out for that would mean that Louise was reacting badly therefore needing medical attention?" I asked, worried that I would miss something and Lou would be in danger.

"I don't expect a problem and I will be coming every day, and her key worker will also visit to make sure she is doing well mentally." Then all at once Louise appeared. "Hi Sandra" she said.

"Hallo Louise are you ready to start?" the nurse asked.

"Oh yes I am so ready," this was a really positive answer and I was very happy that she seemed so upbeat.

The nurse then explained that she needed to ask Louise questions about her drug use, and when she last had heroin.

Expecting her to just answer the questions, I was surprised when Louise told the nurse that she wanted it to be confidential, and that they would go in the other room.

I sat in the kitchen waiting for 1 hour wondering why I was unable to be involved, but apparently because Louise was 16 she had the right to refuse any information being given to us.

When they finally emerged I was told that medication should be given at various times and she would be back the next day.

A large package was then handed to Louise.

The nurse dashed to the front door checking her watch and mumbling that she had another three patients to visit and was late. That was it, my help was five minutes in the kitchen, and a list with the medication wrapped in a carrier bag that Lou plonked on the table top.

As I went through the contents of the bag Louise explained what each packet of pills were for. There was anti-sickness drugs, Imodium for diarrhoea, sleeping tablets, anti-depressants, and the de-tox drugs themselves. I was stunned by the amount that was needed, but at least the treatment was beginning and my daughter would be safe at home with us. That afternoon

Lou started the course of medication, and was unwell almost immediately, so went to bed.

The first night was awful, she was unable to sleep, and she was sweating, and felt very unwell. I spent most of the night in her room with her as I did not want her to feel alone. We did not talk a lot, but as I sat there watching my dear daughter suffer, it reminded me of a distant Christmas long ago.

Louise and her brother were so excited and had helped stuff the turkey and chop the vegetables for the next day. Lou was nine and was putting Ginger the cats Christmas stocking by his bowl, he was never left out and Lou had bought him a fluffy mouse for his present. Both James and Lou went to bed with their pillow cases ready to take whatever Father Christmas was going to leave for them.

Lou had asked for anything Barbie, James on the other hand wanted a chainsaw.

Dawn broke and we were awakened by the sound of whimpering in Louise's bedroom. Poor Lou had got herself so excited she made herself ill and was unwell most of the morning, and so looking at her in her bed shaking, reminded me of that little girl so long ago, wanting her Mum to kiss it better.

The next morning she just wanted to stay in her room, so I accepted this happy in the knowledge that she was in bed resting, and tried to get on with the day.

Ryan had taken the day off to spend time at home and kept popping in to see her. Emma and Holly rang to see if she was allright and find out whether she was coping. James kept his distance.

She wanted her boyfriend to come round but this was definitely a no as we were convinced he was the reason she was in this situation, plus I wanted her to have the best chance of recovery, and not take the risk that he would bring her some drugs. Louise was beginning to suffer from severe withdrawal symptoms, and I was relieved when the nurse arrived. She took her blood pressure and said it was very low so her daily dose was changed. Once again I was not party to her consultation, and Louise and her nurse closed the door for privacy.

There were so many questions I wanted answers to, and when they had finished I ventured to ask if I could have a one to one with the nurse so that my concerns could be addressed. The nurse seemed to be happy to answer some of my queries but pointed out that she was unable to discuss any issues with me without Louise being present, as it would jeopardise her trust in confidentiality.

I was not interested in what was being said in the counselling sessions, I just wanted to know if my daughter was ok and the treatment was not going to give her any other problems.

We were also really concerned that they understood why we felt she needed to be at home with us and safe whilst this detox was going on.

We explained we thought it unwise that she go out alone as we were worried she would take the opportunity to see the boyfriend, and I hoped that they would agree, and tell Louise that it was sensible for her home for the two weeks while she was recovering.

Knowing I wanted to talk about this, it seemed unfair that I should be put in the position of having to talk about her in front of her?

I had now quickly realised that whatever I wanted to say was being ignored as Louise had all the cards in her favour, and if she didn't want me to know anything I was excluded under this confidentiality rule. Whilst I understood that the nurse had no power to stop her seeing him, to my horror, she openly encouraged Louise to go out alone after a few days, when she was feeling better.

Ryan and I offered to take her out and drive her anywhere she wanted to go, but she did not want us with her. Louise then did as we thought she would do and took this as an opportunity to see the boyfriend. We were very worried that he would jeopardise her recovery and bring her drugs, also she was not coping very well physically with the medication so I was concerned that she was being put at risk of collapse.

On day four the social drug worker arrived with the nurse, and as before they went into the other room. I requested that they spoke to me after, they didn't seem happy to do so and the social worker made it quite plain that she would not discuss anything to do with Louise's problem with us, as she was there for Louise and we should get counselling from another source.

I was furious, I was the one that was administering dangerous drugs to my daughter and was responsible with making sure she didn't overdose, and I was the one clearing up the mess and being up with her when she was unwell.

I was the one that had to cope with Louise's mood swings, and yet I had no rights as a mother to ask any questions relating to this illness.

With all the stress of the past few weeks I was beginning to fight the world.

Ryan had noticed a change in me, and it was not for the better.

Not only was he having to work and earn a living, he was also trying to come to terms with it all in his own way, and now he had a ranting wife that was very angry over the whole affair.

When they finally came into the kitchen I decided that whether Louise was there or not, I would let the social worker know, in no uncertain terms that I was not happy with the way that my worries and feelings were being dismissed by them, as I felt I might just as well have not been there.

They gave me all the sympathetic noises but the only person they were interested in was Louise and her progress with the detox, they were not interested in any feedback I might have to offer. I also begged them again to advise that Louise stayed indoors with us for the rest of the two weeks and didn't go out with the boyfriend, as I was so afraid that she would succumb to temptation, plus the added worry that her blood pressure was very low and if she collapsed in the street she could be at risk.

Louise was very upset that I was requesting this and walked out of the room slamming her bedroom door. Well that was a waste of breath because the next day the nurse told Louise to go out and walk with her boyfriend.

I felt was fighting a losing battle against these so called experts, as in our view they were giving her permission to go against good sense. We thought they hadn't got a clue about our daughter, and we had no say in the matter.

I felt I was being used to save money by doing this at home.

The people that knew her as she really was, not the drug addict that she had become needed to know if the counselling sessions had found out why she had started going down this path and what was the real cause, if we knew we could help her recover. If these sessions had come up with anything why could we not be told? Then the penny dropped again, it was up to Louise whether we were informed or not.

By the time we reached the second week, Louise was beginning to get a lot stronger and was feeling a lot better, she informed us she was going out again for a walk and that she was meeting the boyfriend. Apart from physically tying her up, we had to let her go as the nurse had given the go ahead and who were we to argue. At this point I began to realise that Louise had control over this much more than we did and it scared me.

I find it incredible that at sixteen, you can't vote, you can't drive a car, and you are not classed as an adult until your 18, but you can have any procedure done without a parents consent or knowledge.

Also what makes it all right for a parent to administer drugs to their child but to not be told how they are doing, or what may or may not happen?

After much upset and tears we managed to get through the two weeks and Louise emerged unscathed and very positive for the future. I was beginning to see a return of the sweet girl that we had lost for what seemed an age, but at the same time I was not confident that this was indeed the end of our nightmare.

She was ready to go back to work, and the nurse said she would see her once a week also the social worker would be seeing her too.

I was given a leaflet to go to the local drug centre for counselling for us as a family, but after discussing it none of us felt we wanted to go.

Group counselling for one hour would not have helped in our situation we felt.

What we wanted was someone that was in touch with Louise's workers, to advise us, and convey any of our concerns and worries to her workers, that way we were all informed and could share ideas for Lou's recovery plan.

Basically all we were asking for was a link between both parties.

Surely this would not upset the confidentiality rules?

As far as I was concerned, I did not feel ready to speak to a counsellor about my daughter's addiction, because my experience with the professionals up to that moment, had not given me much confidence.

James just blanked out it and refused to talk about it.

He spent a lot of time out with his friends, avoiding too much contact with his sister. He was training to be a car mechanic, and the only way he seemed to be coping with it was to ignore the fact it was happening, and not talk about it.

Then one day he came in and was in tears, it had finally hit him, and this young man suddenly seemed very fragile. He wanted to hit out at someone, and threatened to find the boyfriend to make sure he left Louise alone, I was afraid he was getting out of control. With my determination to get Louise well I had neglected to think about how my other children may be coping with this.

Once again I recognised my failings as a mother to consider all of my children and this was haunting me, and I felt guilty but at the same time could not help having tunnel vision.

James and I sat for a while and he told me that every time he came home he was treading on eggshells as he was frightened that he would explode and say the wrong thing. He could not understand why she was doing this to herself and her family. I was unable to give him any answers and was so sad for him.

He wanted so desperately to help but at the same time could not cope with all of the stress around him.

Luckily he had a good friend at work that talked to him so James at least had someone outside the family to confide in, and I could only hope this would help him to get through it. I was glad of this as my focus was on Louise and my mind couldn't seem to be able to cope with more than one thing at a time.

Louise was getting much better now and I slowly began to calm down, much to Ryan's relief. The treatment seemed to be working and I was sure all we would all begin to heal as a result, and our beautiful daughter would get on with her life and be successful.

Once again I was wrong.

# Chapter 5

It had been two weeks since Louise had come through her detox.

She had returned to work looking fresh and well. Although she looked a lot better and had started to put on a bit of weight, she was still prone to mood swings and insisted that she was out every night seeing her boyfriend.

This really worried me as we knew that he was still taking drugs, but Ryan was quick to point out that we had to start to trust her again. We had tried our best to try and talk to her about this, but she was unwilling to have any word said against him, and so we backed off hoping that she would see sense now that she was clean.

Her workers continued to see her and as far as we knew, she attended all her appointments, so we had no reason to concern ourselves that she wasn't getting the help she needed. Ryan and I, on the other hand, spent most of our time worrying that she was safe as she had to make her own way home every night on the bus. Whether it was the strain of the detox or the fact that Louise was still showing signs of detachment from everyone in the family, after a couple of months, I began to have a strange feeling that all was not well with her, I couldn't put my finger on it but things were not as they should be.

I noticed that Lou's eyes did not look right, her pupils seemed to be very dilated, and I was getting concerned that she was looking pale again.

She never seemed to have any money, and was always coming home late and disappearing upstairs to bed, avoiding us where possible. We would not have any contact with her in the morning as she always seemed to be able to time her disappearance before we got up. Louise was always one step ahead of us.

This was very worrying, but she had all the answers, and I began to doubt my sanity.

I felt it was time that I saw her doctor so that he could explain to me why she was still not getting any better. I made an appointment for us both to see the him when she had her weekly urine sample tested, as I felt that this would be an ideal opportunity to have a good understanding of her on going treatment, and with my input he might consider that he may be missing something.

Louise seemed happy for me to go with her. This was a step in the right direction, for once she was allowing me to be in the surgery when she was seeing the doctor.

We arrived ten minutes early and sat in the waiting room.

Louise was agitated, but I put that down to her nerves.

Then, as her name was called out, I rose from my seat to follow her in when all at once she turned round and in a loud voice said

"I am going in on my own I don't want you there with me because it's my business!"

With that she marched into the surgery and left a very embarrassed mother waiting for her to emerge. I felt so humiliated, I had just been used as a taxi to get her there and was stunned at the outburst that had followed. When she came out I found myself unable to even speak to her, and she was happy to ignore me too.

When I had calmed down I asked why she had done that to me, and without looking at me she answered that I had put too much pressure on her and she could not cope.

"I am concerned about you and just wanted to tell the doctor that you are still suffering side effects," I answered.

After much sighing and shuffling of the feet she looked up and said.

"I wish you would stop fussing, I am ok!" and that ended that conversation.

Over the next few days things began to get worse. She seemed manic in her behaviour sometimes, and then seemed to be quiet. Her manner towards us was still very strained, and I felt that she was hiding something.

I was convinced I was getting paranoid and dismissed these suspicions all the time. Ryan and I were also feeling the strain as we always seemed be talking about Louise and whether she was having problems.

It had become exhausting and we both just carried on not wanting to admit to each other that we were afraid she was back on drugs. Her sisters had started to notice her behaviour too and had expressed their concerns but we were in denial. I think that is the in word at the moment, nevertheless it turned out to be the case.

The weeks turned into months and Louise was getting back to the way she had been before her detox, only this time she was more manic than before.

Her brother couldn't bear to be in her company, and we were getting more and more frustrated with the lack of help from the experts.

I had told her worker that I was convinced that Louise was back on drugs but they refused to talk to me.

On many occasions I rang to inform them of her symptoms, as we had now become accustomed to the signs, but they did not appear to be concerned, and politely reminded us that we had to get information from our daughter as they could not speak to us. Didn't they understand that we were fighting for our baby's life here? We thought we were giving them inside knowledge of our daughter's strange behaviour but they did not seem to us to be listening?

We begged them to try and dissuade Louise from seeing her boyfriend who had by now become the devil incarnate as far as Ryan and I were concerned.

Through all this carnage I was not considering the strain it must have had on her key workers, as they were not allowed to give us any information, so when we demanded answers they were not able to give it must have been just as frustrating for them too, and it was becoming very convenient for me to blame them as well for Louise's problems.

Then one day it reached a head, Louise came in and I decided that we had to ask her the question.

"Louise are you having a problem with drugs again?"

I was afraid of the answer, but needed to know from her lips that I was not paranoid and she was having a problem again.

"It's all right we can help you if you are?" I added, I was convinced that if she were back on heroin she would be confident enough to tell me the truth.

As she turned to me she said the words that I desperately wanted to hear.

"No Mum how could you accuse me of that? I am clean it's just the mood swings that you get after drugs that takes time to go."

This was what I wanted to hear, but at the same time had a feeling Lou was not being honest with me. It was too easy for us to take her word and go against our true gut feelings because the alternative was unthinkable. I chose to believe her as I was still not able to face it, and felt ashamed that I had doubted her.

"Well Louise we are here if you need help at any time, don't be afraid to ever let us know if you have a problem."

"Ok Mum I will," She replied and with that she was out the door to get the bus to meet the boyfriend.

So many opportunities were being missed by us to help Louise, this was caused by our ignorance, and we were just jogging along, accepting all excuses from Louise for her strange behaviour, believing her stories and denying the obvious.

I had not stopped being angry with her workers but I was blinded by the fact that they had their hands tied and whilst I felt they did not understand, they were desperately trying to get Louise to talk to us.

In order to survive drug users have to say and do things they would not normally do, and my daughter was no exception.

She had become very adept at pulling the wool over our eyes, and because we so desperately wanted her to be well we almost always chose to give her the benefit of the doubt.

Although I had tried to believe Lou's last explanation I was still not convinced and I began to become very suspicious of her every move

I started to search her room every time she went out, I looked in her handbag, listened in on telephone conversations were possible, monitored her movements, had friends and family inform on her and the boyfriends whereabouts. We watched her continually. This was becoming a way of life.

On one occasion I found a blackened spoon in her bag and some tin foil, which was also blackened. Not wanting Lou to think I was searching through her things I made out that I had moved her bag and it had dropped out.

I am sure she didn't believe me, but her answer was swift and she explained that it had been in her bag since she was smoking heroin, and she had left it there to remind her never to go back to drugs again.

Yes you guessed it I believed her as it was feasible.

All I seemed to do was worry about her and was unable to switch off.

Sleep had become a luxury as I did not do that very often.

Ryan and I had become distant to each other by now, we just seemed to be dealing with our grief together but in different ways. I felt he didn't talk to her enough, and I didn't stop trying to talk to her.

We wandered around the house avoiding contact, afraid to let our true feelings out. We could not seem to get any help from the key workers, and felt very isolated. Although we were the ones living with this we felt were not important enough to be considered when problems arose.

Then one night Louise did not come home on the last bus.

We didn't know where she was, so we rang the boyfriend.

He was in bed and said he had left her at the bus top as usual.

"Left her at the bus top?" I screamed down the phone.

"Then you went to bed, how caring is that?"

We were so angry with him.

"She is supposed to be your girlfriend and you don't give a toss about her at all, you see her every night."

I was furious this person did not care for her at all.

Then he hit us with a bombshell.

"No she doesn't see me every night I don't know where she is most of the time, she just turns up when she wants too usually at about 9pm." He answered

There was a stunned silence. I was convinced he was lying and I put the phone down.

How naive we were, then all at once Louise appeared at the door with one eye drooping and looking unwell. She walked past us as if we were not there and tried to make her way to the stairs.

"Where have you been?" I cried, running after her.

"I missed the bus and walked," she replied,

"I rang your boyfriend and he was in bed, he does not even make sure you get home safe!" by this time I was really angry and hoped that by pointing this out she may think about it and realise that he did not care about her at all.

"Well he had a bad migraine and I insisted he went to bed otherwise he would have waited with me at the bus stop." She replied with a blank look on her face, and in future don't ring him as his Dad has to get up for work early.

Ryan, on hearing the commotion charged into the room and shouted. "We have to get up in the morning too, and do not appreciate having to wait up for you!"

Once again we were stupid and accepted her excuse but at the same time knew we wanted to believe that she was telling the truth.

I was beginning to think that I was going mad, as I seemed to spend most of my time crying, and confused. In my head the person in front of me had become alien to me. This was not the perfect little girl that loved to cuddle up to me and play with her toys, the child that had made me lovely mothers day cards, and the daughter that was so innocent and loving. It was time to speak to a friend that I hadn't seen for a couple of years, I knew she would be able to help me as she had been through the same thing with one of her sons.

He had been taking drugs since he was eighteen and had been unable to get off them for good. Cathy and I had been friends for 30 years and had been there for each other on numerous occasions. I was very fortunate in having her as a friend as she had never let me down and I trusted her. Having experienced the same as her, I felt very guilty that I had not helped her enough when she had gone through the countless de toxes and relapses that her son had gone through.

It's true what they say you only understand what a terrible impact drug taking has on everyone including the victim, when you go through it yourself.

This was going to be the hardest phone call I would ever make because I did not want to burdon her with my problem and in my heart of hearts knew that she would say what I couldn't say. I decided to send an email that evening and got an immediate phone call from her.

She was in tears, and I was unable to speak to her about it as I was a complete wreck. At the time she called, her son had just been put in prison for stealing a chicken from a supermarket. This was not his first offence, as he had been doing this for some time but I was learning fast the nature of the beast is all consuming, he had to do this to survive, as his habit cost him more money than he had available every day. I was later to discover that Lou had been doing the same. She confirmed the worst to me and I realised that we were not going mad, and suffering from paranoia, our daughter was back on drugs, and it destroyed our world again.

# *Chapter 6*

## THE SECOND COMING

After speaking with my friend both Ryan and I had to face the truth.

Still we did not know what the truth was, although my friend had confirmed that she was probably using again, we still seemed to find it hard to admit it to ourselves. We had begun to see a change in her appearance.

Her hair had become lank and dull, where she normally took pride in her flowing blonde locks. I noticed she was scratching her head a lot, and saw that she also had head lice. She had become quite dishevelled and always seemed to wear the same clothes all the time. Her personal hygiene had also slipped, Louise had always been so meticulous in her cleanliness, but I was beginning to wonder when she had last had a shower.

Louise continued to never have any money, although she earnt very well her wages only seemed to last a week, then she borrowed money from us to see her through the month. When we asked her where it was going she gave us many excuses including paying for nights out with the boyfriend, and paying back money she had borrowed in the past.

Once again the obvious was staring us in the face and I do not understand to this day why we continually believed her. If I had been watching someone else do the same thing for their daughter, I would have asked them why they were lending her money. Looking back it was stupid, but although we suspected she had slipped back into her addiction, we were hoping that Louise was just not managing her wages properly and continued being in denial.

Every answer Lou gave us seemed feasible and so we felt we had to give her the benefit of the doubt, this was beginning to become a habit.

We devised a plan to help her budget properly, we sat her down and wrote a monthly money plan and even offered to hold back cash for her so that at least if she overspent she would have money to fall back on.

Needless to say Louise was not interested in handing any money over to us, as she did not want to lose any control over her finances.

It was clear to me that she would have been too restricted, as she was probably spending all her money on paying debts and dare I say it, drugs.

It's really strange, but after a while I thought I was paranoid, as I was always trying to understand why Lou's behaviour seemed wrong and feared the worst.

I thought maybe I was the one looking for excuses to accuse her of going back to her drug taking, and was ignoring the pleas of innocence

This is the nature of the beast, those words haunted me as they were so true.

The facts are that every excuse that she had given us was very convincing, and so it was very easy to blame ourselves for doubting the person that meant so much to us.

Louise had become a hardened liar, she had learnt to manipulate and control, and with the help and information she received from her drug advisers, had learnt that she did not have to explain herself to us and was in no doubt of her rights. If only we had rights too, but it seemed the more we tried to help the worse it became.

By the time another autumn approached Louise seemed to be in a lot of trouble.

We noticed her behaviour was getting worse, and she seemed to need to be out all of the time, arriving home in the early hours of the morning. Knowing that addiction can put the users into very dark and dangerous places, we decided to confront her and find out what was happening.

The first job was to inform her key workers of our concerns that she may be in trouble, and to let them know that we were worried so we rang and gave them our concerns that Louise was using again, and maybe having problems.

Once again they told us we were not privilege to any information, and that we needed to talk to Louise.

I just did not know where to turn next.

Both Ryan and I decided to speak to her that evening and find out once and for all what she was doing. Then just as we were thinking that this nightmare was never going to end, Louise came home with the nurse that had seen her through her detox.

"I've got something to tell you Mum." She said.

Her nurse sat by her side as if she were shielding her from some terrible fate.

I knew immediately what she was going to say next.

"I am back on drugs" she blurted out.

"I know, Louise" I said.

For a moment both the nurse and Lou sat in silence seemingly surprised at my statement. There were no tears on my part this time, I was quite calm and felt numbed by it all. I looked at her and wondered why she had needed the nurse with her, was I that unapproachable?

I was relieved that she had finally told me but hurt and upset with her for not trusting me enough to tell me sooner. "Where do we go from here?" I dared to ask.

"Well I am putting Louise on methadone and this will stabilise her until she can have another detox." The nurse answered.

"Hold on a minute, when was this decided? I asked, I don't want her on methadone it's as bad as heroin for addiction," I knew from my friends experience that her son had told her that methadone was very hard to be weaned off, as he had been on it for years, and try as he may could not cope with the decrease in dose in order to be detoxed. "Well this is how Louise wants to do it and I feel that this is the right thing for her."

I began to well up inside, this woman once again, had come into my house, dictated to me how my daughters treatment was going to be handled, leaving me feeling like an outsider, these people had discussed and arranged treatment for Louise without any rapport with us or any explanation as to how long it would take to get her clean again.

"I thought you told me you had good results with the method you used in her first detox,"

"Yes we had" answered the nurse, but she was shuffling in her seat.

"How many young people did you cure?" I asked.

The reply filled me with horror,

"Just the one and that was Louise." She replied.

"Out of how many?" I asked.

"Fifteen" she replied.

"And you reckon one good result out of fifteen warrants a statement from you saying that using this method is successful?"

By now I was finding it very hard to keep control.

"Well when I first put Louise on this programme it had been successful with eight other young addicts but they have since re-used"

"Well I think that we can now say that you have had failure with that method, don't you?" I was quick to reply.

Her expression said it all, and I realised I was dealing with someone who was incapable of understanding what I was implying. That made me wonder how much the so called experts actually understood. They may have all the qualifications to administer the medication that is needed, and trained in some sort of counselling, but I felt that we were still in the stages of experimentation where treatment was concerned.

For once I felt proud that I had finally found the strength to confront her.

The nurse was slightly embarrassed at her original declarations of success and had no further answers to give.

Now that the deed had been done the nurse got up and arranged for Louise to get her prescription, and start immediately on her stabilisation.

In the time it took her to leave our drive, Louise had disappeared out the front door to see the boyfriend leaving Ryan and I in utter shock and disbelief over it all.

I rang my other daughters to let them know we were starting all over again to try and rid Lou of this terrible addiction. Both Emma and Holly were not surprised that she was back on drugs as they had suspected her of using for a long time, but like us dared not to believe it. Ryan and I sat watching television that evening and whilst flicking through the channels noticed that drug use was in some programs, being used as a joke, referring to cocaine as Charlie. Comedy programs seemed to make fun of situations where pot smoking was happening.

Normally we would not have taken any notice, but now we had experienced at first hand the consequences of drug abuse, we were horrified.

What chance did the younger generation have if the media were giving the impression that it is acceptable to take the odd soft drug.

Unfortunately it does not stop at soft drugs as they start to become ineffective as time goes by, so more harder drugs are needed to be taken, and this is the nature of the beast.

When we turned to watch the news we were stunned to see stars in the media that were openly admitting using drugs, and seeming to be accepted even when their behaviour showed they were out of control, and with the tabloids showing photographs of obvious drug abuse I was thinking, these people were so privileged, they had enough money to feed their addictions, and at the same time had enough to get into exclusive re-hab therapy, unlike many addicts.

Everywhere we looked it was staring us in the face. We could not get away from drugs. I realised that we are in a pandemic situation, and it is getting worse because there is no vaccine for this disease.

It was about this time that a talented singer and her boyfriend were in the news, clearly in trouble. Once again some of the media were making jokes of the situation, but what kind of message where they sending to their fans I wondered? I was filled with sorrow at the thought of what the families must have been going through, especially seeing they're child battling through addiction with the world being witness to the self-destruction that was unfolding in front of them. I wondered what help they were getting and whether they were falling apart as we were.

It just goes to show that because this has been going on for such a long time maybe it has become the norm and the general public and government alike accept that people will take drugs, so nothing has been done to really tackle it.

I had read that Portugal and some other countries had a different approach to addiction, apparently they have legalised some drug use, and have many re-hab centres giving support to addicts and help encourage them to become clean.

At the same time those that are not ready to de-tox are given the drugs needed in a safe environment in order to keep them stable and safe.

If some drugs were legalised here maybe it would make a difference as long as the backup services were there to help. I wondered if it would help stop the crime syndicates profiting from exploiting the vulnerable, or make things worse.

Whatever the answer was, I did not have it, and felt very inadequate.

The next morning I was just off to visit my parents when the phone rang, it was one of my neighbours informing me that she had seen Louise and her boyfriend in the village shouting and displaying very strange behaviour.

I was horrified, not only was she here in the village without my knowledge, but making it known to everyone that was in earshot that they were on something.

I flew out of the door and got in the car to find her. I did not have to look far as both her and the boyfriend were sitting in the park still arguing, and clearly either drunk or stoned.

As I marched over to them I felt the eyes of a few of my neighbours following my every footstep. Louise looked up and realised that she was in trouble, and the boyfriend suddenly disappeared head first into the bushes.

"Get in the car!" I demanded as I neared her, and expecting a challenge, I got up close to her face and whispered that if she did not do as I wished immediately, she would be in serious trouble with me. I was very surprised that she did not try and argue with me, so I managed to get her in the car and drove her back home.

Once indoors she broke down sobbing that she had an argument with the boyfriend and had lost her temper with him. I just prayed that it was over between them and tried not to show it. She went up to her room and I left her alone knowing that now most of our friends the village would be wondering why Louise was acting so strangely. When Ryan came in he was once again confronted with the latest news of our daughters exploits. We looked at each other, Ryan shaking his head and frowning as the strain of it all had really become too much for him and he disappeared upstairs to his study.

# *Chapter 7*

## THE PAY OFF

*S*till reeling from the news I had received the previous day and getting over the antics from Louise and the boyfriend, I decided to tell her brother that she was going to be stabilised and warned him that she was again trying to cope, until she was able to be detoxed again.

James was sickened and couldn't understand why she was still doing it.

He could not talk to her, and kept his distance as much as possible.

They had never been very close as children being such different characters, so we were not surprised at his response. James had always strived to be the best and wanted to do well in business. He had used his dyslexia as an advantage as he always thought out of the box. His was why I felt he was unable to allow himself to be side tracked by what he described as someone that was doing this to herself.

Emma and Holly were also finding it very hard. Holly became very angry, and also didn't want to talk to her. Emma on the other hand wanted to help but like Holly, was concerned about Ryan and me and how we were coping.

I on the other hand was beginning to feel so tired and seemed to cry all the time.

I couldn't function properly, just existing from day to day.

Unfortunately my father had become very unwell and my mother and I were concerned about him too. I had told my parents about the problems we were having with Lou, and my Dad who had always been the rock of the family, was so worried and baffled by the whole thing, that I always tried to be positive in front of him. My mother was very good and listened to me rant on about the situation. Never blaming Louise, but distraught at the thought of her going through this terrible time again, mum could only be there for me, as I had always tried to be there for Lou.

Every Thursday I took my mother shopping and the journey took about one hour. In that time the whole conversation would be either my Dad's health or Louise's problem, it helped both of us to off load to each other.

Dad had been short of breath for a long time and was undergoing tests to find out the exact cause of his health problem. He had also lost weight and was very tired and unable to walk too far before he would have to sit down. I was very concerned about him as I was worried that they were going to find a tumour.

I think that because I had been so pre-occupied with Lou, I had put all other problems on a back burner, and had neglected to face up to other issues within the family.

Then one day in November Louise came home in a terrible state, she had been threatened at the bus stop by some dealers. Her hands were dirty, and grazed, she was also showing signs of a swelling on her cheek that was red, and she was shaking all over with a tear stained face. My daughter seemed so afraid and it took a lot of persuasion from us before she confessed that she owed money to drug dealers and they had sent some rough characters to intimidate her to make sure she understood that they were serious about the debt.

A car containing these louts had driven up onto the pavement pinning her to the wall threatening to kill her if she didn't pay up in twenty four hours.

They had been waiting outside her workplace as they had been following her in order to get the message across, and they had.

At last Louise was opening up to us, but I was so frightened for her.

Her Dad managed to find out how much was owed and it came to just over one thousand pounds.

"We will pay them off, but they will understand that it will be a one and only payment, there will be no more." Her Dad announced. Ryan's sudden statement surprised me but I was so proud of him as once again he was taking charge and doing what he could to help our daughter. I was reminded of the reasons I married him, like my father, he was strong when it came to family, and through all this hell I had forgotten how important it was for us both to be constant with each other.

In our grief we had both got on with trying to cope in our own way, not daring to get too close as we hurt so much. We both thought we would never be happy again, how could we? Our family was near to breaking point, James continued to be angry and distant, Emma having the task of looking after her children as well as supporting us was forever calling to make sure we were allright, Holly worried but not wanting to be too involved as she was fed up with the whole situation, and we all felt that there was nowhere to go to get the help we all so desperately needed.

Louise wanted to pay the dealers on her own as she did not want to involve her father, but her Dad was insistent, "You will not be alone, we will both meet them, as I want to make sure they understand that you are not alone."

Ryan then went to the police to inform them of what he was about to do.

He did this hoping that they would be able to be in the background so that they would know who these dealers were and would be able to arrest them and stop them from profiting out of other addicts misery. The police advised Ryan to be in a public place, and look the dealer straight in the eyes, being very precise in his language when speaking to him. This was very surprising to me as I would have thought that they would have wanted to arrest these dealers immediately, but they did not seem interested. They explained that the fact that Ryan was giving them money did not prove anything so we were alone.

They also knew who the dealers were but had to catch them in the act before a case could be upheld against them. Ryan took their advice, but confessed to me that he was really worried about the meeting as he was ready to attack the dealer and teach him a lesson he would not forget for threatening his daughter.

Lou made the arrangement for them to meet in the middle of town, to pay the money off.

It was market day and very busy. As they waited outside the clock tower Ryan noticed a black BMW slowly drive by and park fifty yards down the road.

The windows were tinted and the car had obviously had a lot of money spent on it as there were spoilers, and large exhaust pipes protruding from the rear.

No-one emerged from the car but from another direction a tall thin scruffy young man walked up to them. Ryan looked at the approaching man, who he guessed was the dealer, and was trying to memorise the pinched features and piercing empty eyes. The man stared at Ryan and said nothing.

Louise was trembling and unbeknown to her, so was her father not with fear but with anger.

"This is all there will be and now the debt is paid in full, there will be no more, and you will stay away from her."

Ryan had found his voice and was very precise in his manner. As he spoke, Louise moved closer to her father and touched his arm for comfort. This gave Ryan the confidence to just stand there and look into the cold menacing face of the dealer. The dealer looked at Lou, and smirked.

Without saying a word the dealer looked in the envelope, and nodded to Ryan.

Ryan, by now wanted to attack this creature in front of him but good sense prevailed and he held it in.

As the dealer walked away, Ryan noticed a burly man step out of the parked car and take the envelope from him before driving off.

The dealer skilfully disappeared into the crowd.

Louise then came home with her father, and we decided then that she would have to leave her workplace as it was too risky for her to work there anymore.

If you have a problem with drugs it is not feasible to work with money and we were concerned that she may have been tempted to take money for her debts.

I had been worried for a long time that she may have been forced into prostitution by theses evil men to pay for her habit, but I could not contemplate that as it would be too much to bear.

I had read about girls having to survive by shop lifting, and after being caught had no option but to resort to selling their bodies. I would rather pay for her drugs than have the thought of my beautiful daughter going through that. After the drama we sat down for the first time in a long time and talked about her addiction.

She admitted to us that she had in fact been on methadone longer than we thought and that was why I had been stopped from going in to see her doctor months earlier. The dose had not been high enough for her to cope with her cravings, as she was still using heroin as well as having her methadone.

I remember thinking that this confidential nonsense had put the doctor, nurse, and key workers in the unenviable position of having to lie to me about her medication, giving Lou utmost power in this situation, that cannot be right.

She was now on a higher dose of methadone and was feeling better she said.

And then it clicked in my mind and it filled me with fear.

The reason she had told us that she was using again was because she could not get any more drugs as she owed so much, and she was being threatened with beatings and God knows what else, her only refuge was methadone, and seeing her nurse again she was able to start on an increased dose.

It worried me that this recovery was temporary as she may not have been ready to give up drugs, she just wanted a quick fix to keep her stable, and she was just fooling herself.

A mother's instinct is never wrong and I really wanted to be wrong this time.

We talked about the boyfriend and although they had now made up after the drama in the park, we decided that she should stay away from him as she needed to get better and he was still using. We hoped that she would understand that we needed her to be away from all previous contacts to give herself every chance to get well again.

Louise agreed to our terms which gave us hope that at last she was serious about her recovery. There was a computer course that her key workers felt would be a good distraction for he, and at the same time help her to get some sort of qualification when she was ready to work again.

She agreed to do the course, and as it was in another town I would be the one to take her there and back.

We were not ready to trust her to go on her own as we were afraid she would meet up with the drug dealers again, and the debt now paid would mean she could be able to get more heroin.

She also surprisingly said she would stay at home with us for three months under our rules to build up trust with us. Thinking back she would have said anything to keep us happy, and have a safe place to live with no more threats.

We felt that keeping her home with us, although it would be very hard for her, was the only way we could make sure she did not fall back into the old routine, and for a while she stuck to the rules.

# *Chapter 8*

## LIES AND DECEIT

*O*ver the next couple of months calm reigned in our household, I drove Louise back and forth from the chemist to take her methadone every day.

This was a very difficult thing for her to have to do as she had to wait in the chemist while they checked her prescription, wait while they mixed it, and then have to take it in front of the pharmacist. I had noticed that she always seemed agitated when going so on one occasion I went in with her.

The attitude from the counter staff towards her and others that were waiting their turn was to say the least uncomfortable. Whilst I could understand the prejudice about drug using, addiction after all is an illness, a recognised illness, I felt therefore these professionals should understand that and act accordingly.

Where once I had looked down on these people, I realised I had not thought about the dealers being the low life's, and the users the victims.

I felt ashamed at my own prejudices and wanted to shout out to all in the chemist that my daughter was ill and did not need to be made to feel like an outcast.

After that I made sure I went in with her and stood by her as she was shunted round the back to take her methadone. Louise was doing well with her computer course, and she seemed to look forward to going. It gave us hope that she had finally turned the corner. The boyfriend had not been mentioned and I had stopped crying. James was beginning to talk to her again and the family as a whole seemed to be settling down.

It was approaching Louise's 18th birthday and her older sister Emma had promised to take her out around the town, we had begun to relax the rules a bit and allow Louise to meet up with her friends for a few hours a week.

I continued to drive her to anywhere she needed to go, or to her friend's house as I was trying to trust in her again.

Just before her birthday outing I had dropped her off at the computer centre as usual and then went around the corner to get some shopping.

As I drove off I saw a familiar figure behind a car appear and go into the building. Suddenly I felt very nauseous, it was the boyfriend, and they were meeting each other when I dropped her off. As I sat in the car out of sight I watched them go hand in hand into the park.

He looked very thin and pale he was obviously still using and then I realised that I had to do something to stop her going back down that destructive path.

I decided to pick her up as usual and wait til we got home to confront her.

I had already rung her father to let him know we were in for a battle but we were both resolute in our decisions not allow her to see him.

As you can imagine it was not a pleasant meeting and Louise tried everything she could to try and convince us it was a one off meeting.

Then I said it.

"Do you want to get better?" I said calmly

"Yes Mum" she answered

"Well if you see him again while we are trying to get you well I am afraid you will have to leave home and live with him elsewhere, because your father and I cannot continue with all the lies you keep giving us."

I couldn't quite believe that my mouth had said those words but they had, and one thing that all our children understood was that if we made a decision we would stick to it, so I was confident she would not go against our rules.

Her 18th birthday came and she went out with Emma and a couple of friends.

They dressed her up and I was so pleased that she would be having a good time on her special birthday, and as far as we were concerned she was again trying to do everything right.

A couple of weeks passed and once again we noticed Lou was agitated on occasion. I put it down to her trying to not do or say the wrong thing, she was treading on eggshells and I knew it was very hard for her. In the meantime my father had been given the bad news that he had terminal lung cancer, but with treatment they could help him and hopefully prolong his life by radiation and chemotherapy.

This had come as a terrible shock to us all, including Lou.

My Mum was beside herself, but was determined to stay positive, and keep dad well.

I was commuting back and forth helping my mother to look after him as he was too weak to get in and out of the bath alone.

Never losing his sense of humour I arrived one evening to help with his bathing.

As I entered the bathroom I was surprised by the sight of my father sitting on the side of the bath, with flippers on his feet and wearing a snorkel, saying the words Dive, Dive, Dive, with the sound of a submarine coming from my mother's lips. It was wonderful to really laugh again, and for once the tears were of happiness not sorrow. He always asked how everything was going and being the same as everyone else in situations that are not ideal I answered "Don't worry Dad its ok"

Louise had been restricted for 4 months and was now stir crazy so we started to allow her to come and go on her own again as we were confident that she was all right, maybe still a bit manic sometimes but we couldn't keep her in forever.

Over the next few weeks she seemed to go out more and more.

Her attitude had begun to change again, but I was so engrossed in my father's illness that I concentrated on him more than Louise.

James had begun to distance himself a bit too and I couldn't understand why.

He was still very angry with her, and he just didn't want to be in the same room as her. Also James had started to go out all the time and seemed very unhappy.

I knew I would have to confront him and tell him that he needed to forgive her and try to talk about it more. His reply stunned me.

"How can you ask that of me when I go to work every day, don't take drugs don't drink and I am trying to be the best I can at my work, and Louise is always the one that has the help and attention from everyone!"

I looked at him and just felt so guilty.

I had assumed he was ok and because I was so wrapped up in Louise's addiction and my father's illness, had forgotten that there was another person in the household that was trying to cope with the devastation of it all.

I had all the support I could wish for from my family and friends, even the neighbours that had witnessed Louise in the village acting in a drunken manner, stood by us as people were generally concerned.

James on the other hand wanted to be a support but he was witnessing first-hand the upset that it was causing us and he felt totally helpless. As I walked over to my son his eyes welled up, all I could do was hold him close and tell him how proud we were of him and that we knew he was hurting too. He clung to me for what seemed an age, and he sobbed in my arms for the first time.

I felt it was good that he finally released his hurt and anger, and I hoped that this would make him realise that it was not his fault that

Louise was taking drugs, he had not the power to stop her, nor had we.

He then told me that he had seen Louise with the boyfriend the evening before.

I was stunned but until I had the proof, I wanted to believe he was mistaken.

My eldest daughter Emma came round and spent time with James in the hope of getting him to open up more. Holly was very worried that events were taking a turn for the worse again and also came over to spend time with James. As a family we were determined that we were going to survive this and Louise would be well. All thoughts of failure were dismissed from my mind as I recalled my friend's son had over seven detoxes and had still gone back to drugs.

His mother had gone to all his meetings, seen his counsellors, been with him in court, had fought for help for him, and still he was not well.

This had been going on for 20 years.

The only comfort I had was that as far as I was concerned Louise was not going to be like that as he started taking drugs because he witnessed a family tragedy and so needed to escape the pain of that. My daughter was not like other users and there was no reason in my mind for her to do this, she must have just been unlucky and got hooked up with the wrong person and so we would not have to worry about her getting well because she was going to get better!

We had also been down the 'where did we go wrong' guilty thoughts, and we knew that it was not our fault either. It was definitely the boyfriends fault for getting her hooked in the first place as far as we were concerned. What happened over the next few days will be etched in our memories until the day we die.

Ryan and I were again noticing strange behaviour from Louise. Her room had become a tip, her appearance was not as good as usual, she was losing weight, she did not want to talk to us, and her eyes began to droop sometimes on one side. As this had happened before I was really concerned. Every time I mentioned this to her she had an excuse that it was after effects of drug use.

Every time she gave an excuse I swallowed it because that is what I wanted to hear. I began to panic and fall apart again.

A friend of mine insisted that I go to see a drug councillor and the appointment was made. She worked in the same office that Louise used for counselling, and so I had first-hand knowledge of the building. There were a few obvious users on the steps leading to the office, they did not intimidate me I felt numb at the sight of them. As I entered the office I was met by a jolly lady and asked to take a seat in the interview room. I sat alone for what seemed an age when the door opened and a lady dressed very much like a hippie entered. I was not impressed and did not intend to talk to this woman about my inner thoughts, and was determined to get off my chest my disgust at the way there was no help for families going through this hell. Well that didn't last long, I opened my mouth to say something and all I could do was sob. I was so cross with myself, I had intended to be so calm but as usual my plans had gone pear shaped.

I did manage in the end to let vent over how I felt about my daughters detox, and to be fair she tried to explain why there was not a lot of help for parents, and the confidentiality act was not a help, but that did not change the situation.

The meeting ended up with my eyes red raw and puffy, the poor woman must have wondered what had hit her, and I was convinced that it had been a waste of time that would not be repeated.

When I arrived home it was early evening and Louise was not eating much again, so I decided to call her nurse and key worker to inform them that I had worries that she was using again, may have anorexia, did not want to show her arms so was probably self-harming, and generally slipping back into her old ways.

Needless to say I was told that they would not discuss with me anything about my daughter, and that I should speak to her.

Later that evening when Louise disappeared again I decided to look in her room for evidence, under her bed I found three bottles of half full methadone, as she was only given enough for two days there was too much there.

When she arrived home she said that the chemist had given her too much so that was why she had some left. Yes I swallowed that excuse, of all the stupid excuses I had heard that was the best, but I truly believed her.

Well she went out again and I went over to my parent's house to help bath my Dad. It is strange that by helping my mother, the burden of what was happening at home was less intense. My father was about to start radio-therapy.

This meant we would be travelling to and from a hospital every day for four weeks and I would be driving him there, but it was all right, as he was so upbeat and never lost his sense of humour, so it ended up being a kind of respite for me.

When I got home after the latest trip, the worst news hit me as I walked in the door. Louise had been spotted by two people with the boyfriend in the town and they were both obviously under the influence of drugs.

Ryan and I had to decide whether to make the terrible decision to make our daughter homeless as we felt we had to carry out the threat that had been a condition of her recovery. Tough love is the in phrase I think, well that was true, but the tough love was our heartache.

# *Chapter 9*

## TOUGH LOVE

*W*hen Louise was in bed Ryan and I spent most of the night talking about how we were going to carry out this terrible deed. We were absolutely devastated at the prospect of making our daughter homeless. We had nowhere to turn, no amount of advice could have helped with this dilemma.

We had long stopped recognising this girl that was in our house, she had become a stranger to us.

The worst of it was that every time I looked at her I saw my dear little girl, colouring in her books, playing with her friends, cuddling up to us on the sofa whilst watching Sesame Street. Where was my dear Louise? She had gone from our lives. Would we ever get her back again? I remembered the time she went out to play in the park and there was a thunder storm, she had come running home in floods of tears frightened that she would be struck by lightning.

Her friends had all laughed at her calling her a baby and in her panic she had wet herself.

By the time she eventually got home she was hysterical, I did not know what had occurred, and ended up having to raise my voice to get her to stop crying.

I just did not know what had happened to make her so frightened.

Through her sobs she managed to tell me what had occurred.

As I held her trembling body, she felt so fragile and I was determined that this precious child would never feel fear like that again. I just wanted to put my arms around my little girl again but she wasn't there. This person that I had living in our house was not known to me and the loss I felt was getting greater.

Louise had again become a very cold unfeeling person she seemed to have no desire to give up this horrible existence.

The dawn came and Ryan decided to take control of the situation. I was relieved as I could not do this alone. It was 8am and he walked into Louise's room and told her we knew she was still using drugs and that she had been seen with the boyfriend. Expecting a tirade of denials Ryan waited for her response.

There was no answer from her, she just stared out of the window.

"We told you that if you continued to lie to us, you would have to leave so pack your things you are leaving today."

Her father said it in a very calm way I thought

Whether it was the shock of what her father had said or the fact that all feelings were numb from the drugs, she said nothing, got up, and slowly started to pack some clothes in a case.

I was distraught, the tears flowed freely, what where we doing? were we making the biggest mistake ever?

I went up to my sons room and informed him of what was happening so that he could say goodbye.

"You're doing the right thing Mum." He said, but at the same time was in shock over the events that were unfolding.

We had decided to call her key workers to inform them that we were going to drop Louise off at the local centre just so that they were aware she was a vulnerable girl alone in the town. As they were such experts and did not feel we had anything to offer with her recovery, I felt it time that they took responsibility of her welfare, and they could now look after her.

Ryan was cold and unfeeling with his language and told them that they would have to re-house her as she was now homeless.

"We can't do that," said the stunned key worker.

"Well it is down to you now to sort something out as we can no longer do this, my wife and I refuse to watch our daughter destroy herself and her family."

With that he informed them that he would be there in an hour and to make sure someone was in attendance. Then he put the phone down and proceeded to help Louise gather her belongings.

By now I was pacing the kitchen floor, not knowing what to do.

My daughter was being thrown out of her home by us, her parents with no prospect of living accommodation. The only thing that made me feel better was that she had been paid some money by her aunt three days earlier, so would have enough to at least stay in a bed and breakfast for a few days. I was to find out later that she had already spent it and would be sleeping in the local public toilets that night.

Then came the moment for her to leave, I was near to collapse and was finding it very hard to stay calm. As Louise walked out of the door she did not look at me, say anything, or show any emotion. It was clear to me that she had not understood what was happening and for a moment I wanted to stop and say no to this eviction. Ryan was on auto pilot and just doing the deed.

James was relieved but worried for her, and he avoided seeing her waiting til she had left. I was on the brink of mental exhaustion.

As the car disappeared from the drive, I suddenly felt a terrible physical pain travel through my body.

I had never experienced anything like it before or since.

It was as if all the grief had come to a head in that instance, and I was unable to control my feelings.

James gave me a hug and left for work saying "It's the right thing Mum." she needs to be shocked into getting clean. The silence that was left in the house as James drove out of the drive was almost too much to bear. I went straight up to my daughter's room and sobbed at the sight of the empty bed and drawers.

I sniffed her bedclothes trying to recapture the essence of my dear Lou, but just got the smell of a stranger.

The only thing I could do was clear out every part of that person from the room so set about emptying everything I could find out of the room and put the last of her belongings in black bags. I was like a woman possessed, everything was going, the more I found the more manic I became I just wanted to clear the room of the person that had left because she was not my daughter.

My sobs became uncontrollable and the guilt I was feeling was unbearable.

Under the bed I found methadone bottles again, in the cupboards there was evidence of drugs, the more I found the angrier I became.

Her 18th birthday cards were in the cupboard with one from the boyfriend.

That was immediately destroyed.

I was half way through and Ryan walked in the room, red eyed and looking exhausted.

"I dropped her off and it was terrible to see her there alone," he sighed

My brave husband had once again been there to take control of the situation, but all I could do was continue to clear out the room while Ryan went into his study and closed the door. I did not enter his study as he needed to be alone with his grief, and I needed to cleanse the house of our despair.

How could we ever be happy again, how could life continue, had we condemned our daughter to death by shutting her out, were we doing it for the right reasons? These questions were going round in my head. One thing was for sure Louise was taking drugs and going to dangerous places when she was living at home, so any risks that she took were happening whether she was here or not.

We had not abandoned her through our inability to cope but because we loved her so much we had to do something to make her turn her life around, although we did not have much faith in that idea.

I would never have imagined that we would ever do this to one of our precious children and had frowned on others for doing the same, and I was afraid we had made the worst decision we could ever have made. I spent all day in the room and after it was cleared and cleaned I closed the door determined to not go in there again.

Ryan by now had emerged from his study, we were unable to speak we just sat in the lounge in silence wondering if she was allright, and wishing someone could have told us we were right in our actions.

Her workers surely would help her, we were trying to convince ourselves, but we did not know if they would.

# *Chapter 10*

## THE AFTERMATH

*R*yan was truly a broken man. This had been such a shock to him. Once again he had been unable to save his daughter from this horror, and he felt a failure.

In his mind fathers should be there not only to support their children but to be able to fix everything. Convinced he had not been a good dad, he blamed himself for Louise's predicament and was tormented over the way he had to physically evict his daughter into the unknown.

He began spending more time alone in his study and try as I may, was unable to reach him.

I was just functioning and going about my daily tasks without feeling anything.

The everyday routine was carried out and the numbness inside was becoming a comfort to me, as it blocked out the reality of our situation. I continued ferrying my parents back and forth to the hospital, but was unable to confide this time.

After a couple of days, Ryan decided to call Louis's key worker one more time to make sure they were with her and she was safe, so he dialled the number and waited for some reassurance. On asking for information he was told that they had been in contact with Louise but they were unable to discuss the issue any further. No change there then.

We were left feeling guilty and desolate, praying that we had done the right thing. If only there were someone that could tell us what to do, but there was no help, we had to live with our decision. Our two other daughters when informed of the events that had occurred made all the right noises.

"It was the right thing to do" they both concurred.

They had been such a support and I was grateful to have both of them on our side. They in turn had not been able to understand why we continually believed the stories that Lou was giving us, and both were frustrated because they knew that she was getting worse in front of our eyes. What they did not realise was that we did know but were in denial again.

For the next few days both Ryan and I still walked around in a daze, not saying much to each other in case we said the wrong thing, we tip-toed around not daring to mention Louise. James began coming over to me on occasion and giving me a hug saying he was here for us too. I wondered how long he had waited to be able to feel he could help us as well. I told him I was so grateful he was there.

The longing for my dear daughter was getting more painful and I became worried that I was on the edge of some sort of breakdown.

Our neighbour had also known about our problem and she came round to try and help both Ryan and I to come to terms with the last week's events

Being a nurse she recognised that I was on the brink of total breakdown, and warned me of this. I took her advice and made an appointment to see my doctor, who happened to be Lou's physician as well.

I did not know what to say to him or what he could do about how I felt.

One thing was for sure I was not going to go on any anti-depressants, so cancelled at the last minute and decided to soldier on.

The time had also arrived to start taking my father for more chemotherapy, so I took a deep breath and decided that I had to tell all as I had run out of excuses when asked where Louise was and how she was doing. I was surprised that I managed to tell them without floods of tears, was I becoming hardened to this or had my mind taken such a battering I was no longer capable of emotion?

Well after that I started to focus on my father and I began to stop thinking about Louise and just concentrated on his treatment. Ryan started to bury himself in his work so we continued to be strangers in our own home.

A month passed and I had just come back from my parents house when Ryan met me at the door. "Get yourself ready we are going out to dinner!" he announced. To say I was surprised was an understatement, it had been so long since we had spent any time together, let alone gone out.

He had made a reservation at a local restaurant, and we sat looking at the menu, trying to make conversation not daring to mention Lou. After a while we started to talk about the way we were both carrying this burden and to my surprise Ryan said that as far as he was concerned Louise was not on his mind anymore and that he felt more at peace since she had been gone.

I had to admit that I felt the same, we were both detaching from the worry of it all and not having her around, and not knowing what she was doing became a relief to us both. As the evening progressed we found ourselves beginning to relax, and all the old feelings that had been buried for so long began to emerge again. It was then that I knew we were going to survive this, whatever the outcome, together.

Days went into weeks then weeks turned into months, life was continuing and we had settled down to a more calmer existence. Thoughts of drug taking and all the lies and deceit had become a distant memory, life was better but not yet perfect.

James had met a new girlfriend, and Holly had moved in with her fiancé and was looking forward to getting married in Australia. I had even managed to spend some time with my grandchildren and Emma. All we ever wanted was to have our family settled, this was not going to happen yet I felt.

Just when we were not expecting it I had a phone call from a friend saying that Louise was sleeping rough in a garden in a tent. She had not moved in with the boyfriend and she was in a hopeless situation. I was stunned, her boyfriend was not with, her then I thought, she must be alone, This was too much to bear and as soon as Ryan came home from work it was decided that she would have to come home.

We could not have her in the house as the rules were still the same but we decided to buy a caravan and have it in the garden so she would be safe and warm. We knew she was still taking drugs as well as methadone so felt vindicated in our decision to make her build up trust and prove that she was going to make the effort to get herself clean. Through our eldest daughter we made contact and she agreed to our terms, once again the boyfriend was not mentioned and we assumed that it was over between them.

The caravan was delivered and placed at the bottom of the garden.

Ryan connected the electricity to the mains and we got some gas bottles for her so we were confident that she would have a real home from home there and be able to cook for herself. We put a television in the dining area and gave it a really good clean. After stocking up the cupboards with food I was really looking forward to her coming home and was proud that we had managed to make a lovely place that she could call her own.

I waited nervously for Emma to arrive with our precious daughter.

Ryan was tinkering in the garden shed when the moment arrived.

The person that emerged from the car was pale and thin, very scruffy in appearance, and looking tired and sad.

There were no hugs or kisses, just a "Hallo Mum, can I have a bath ?"

"Yes of course" was the reply

With that she disappeared up the stairs leaving me holding three bags of smelly clothes. Emma hugged me saying, "Give her time to get settled Mum, she will be ok."

Louise seemed underwhelmed at the caravan but I put that down to her probably being angry with us for making her homeless, but I hoped that she would settle down and get a part time job to help her get back to the real world.

It was late summer and the days were still warm, but Louise always kept her arms covered, I was convinced she was still self-harming and this became a real concern, but at least she was with us and we hoped that her recovery would not be long.

"Anyone sitting there?" I was brought back to the present with a start, and was confronted with a well-spoken smart lady and what I can only describe as a strange looking young man with black eyeliner and multiple piercings.

His clothes would not have been out of place in a Hammer Horror Vampire movie, I think the look is called Goth. I assumed he was her son.

"No" I replied, trying not to stare at the tall figure beside her.

With that they both plonked themselves down beside me and began to tell me all about they're excitement at being invited to the evenings events.

I was also told how they got there, where they parked, and what they were going to do afterwards.

To my surprise the Goth was very well spoken, and polite, offering me one of the sandwiches that had been placed on our table.

"The catering students did the refreshments, I hope they have vegetarian" said the young man as he lifted the bread and inspected the fillings.

The hall was really beginning to fill now and in between mouthfuls of egg and cress the lady that had arrived with the Goth proceeded to tell me how many awards her son was going to be given.

Trying not to lose the will to live I was grateful when another couple sat opposite and started to talk to them. I did feel a bit guilty at not putting myself out to be pleasant but I had other things on my mind, and found myself going back to Louise and the awful vision I had of her when she was in the caravan.

She had been living in the caravan for one month when I had the family come to visit. Holly and Emma arrived and James also had some of his friends over and we were having a really good time. Laughter was back in our house and we all just spent time being like we always were, a happy family though minus one.

As they left I looked down the garden and saw Louise looking through the window of her caravan.

I had not realised she was there as she would normally be out all day. I could just make out her face as she stared down the garden at the house with a really sad expression. I suddenly felt very cold and sick, It was as though my daughter was on the outside looking in. I had not thought to check if she was in the caravan, so she had not been included in the day's events.

This was terrible the thought that she had been forgotten by me was unforgivable as she must have felt so isolated.

She looked very alone and fragile, how could I have forgotten her? how long had she been there just watching from afar?

My immediate thought was to run to her and bring her indoors, but it was too late, the damage had been done.

Then the face at the window was gone, and the child that I yearned to have back disappeared from view, and all at once the grief returned and I went upstairs and sobbed alone.

# *Chapter 11*

## REVELATIONS

*I* had once again begun to notice Louise disappearing at the crack of dawn and arriving back at the caravan late at night, the old pattern had started to evolve again and although both Ryan and I tried to ignore it, hoping it would stop, in our heart of hearts we knew we were fooling ourselves.

Where she was going was a mystery and we were afraid to ask knowing we would only have lies again.

When she left each morning I watched her disappear through the side gate and down the road. This thin pale crumpled young woman's stance was very hunched, and she seemed to hurry as if her life depended on getting to her destination as quickly as possible.

I started to look in the caravan when she was out and once again methadone bottles were found half empty, and there was evidence of drug abuse all over the caravan. I had by now started to recognise the silver paper, discoloured spoons, black marks and ash that give away heroin use.

Also I had at last admitted to myself that chemists do not give too much methadone, so Louise had not needed it.

What some users do is sell methadone in order to buy heroin.

Whether she was doing this or not was a mystery to us.

All I knew was that our daughter, this stranger, had only one priority, and that was where she was going to get her next fix. I decided to go back to the local drug assistance centre in town to try and find out if there were any other parents or advisers that I could talk to about living with drug addiction.

As I approached the building again I was greeted with the usual cold empty stares from the few youngsters sitting in the foyer, and made my way to the reception. There were posters all over the place talking about all manner of addictions, where to get needles, group therapy for addicts, sexual advice, information about HIV, hepatitis, so many but nothing for parents.

The receptionist looked up and I ventured to ask the question.

"Good afternoon, my daughter is a heroin addict and we are having some concerns about her, and I was just wondering if there was any way we could discuss our worries with a mediator that would have contact with her key workers and because of confidentiality rules, no-one will discuss her progress with me."

I knew the answer would be the same as it always was and I was not disappointed.

"I am sorry but we cannot provide any mediator, and I suggest you talk to your daughter, or come along to one of our meetings." She answered.

I thanked her and turned to leave.

As I walked through the foyer a short stocky man came up to me, he looked very drained, for a moment I was concerned that he may be a drunk or drug addict and was about to threaten me. My fears were foundless as he softly whispered to me.

Please forgive me but I overheard your conversation with that lady, and my wife and I are going through the same thing at the moment with our son, and we don't know where to turn."

His face was drawn and looked desperate, and I immediately recognised the despair in his eyes. He then beckoned his wife over and she smiled at me holding out her hand, I took it and introduced myself.

They started to tell me that they're son was sixteen, and had started glue sniffing when he was twelve. He had run away from home and had got involved with the wrong crowd.

He began his downward journey by smoking dope, then taking amphetamines, and after they became ineffective moved on to heroin and cocaine.

It was a very familiar story, and these people had not had the support they needed either.

"We come here in the hope that we will be able to persuade our son to get clean, but when he is here he always refuses to see us and we have no say in the matter." I felt so sorry for them and angry that other parents were also facing the same problems that we had been up against.

"He is only sixteen" his wife added, "he's my only child and I can't bear it!"

We sat in the foyer and compared the experiences we had both encountered.

Like us they had found it very difficult and frustrating, and like me were very angry at the lack of information. I felt so helpless and all I could do was wish them well and hope that one day their son would come to them for help.

I returned home and told Ryan of my encounter at the centre.

At least Louise was living here so we could see her, and know that she had a warm bed to sleep in. Evening fell and a familiar face appeared at the window. Louise had come home early and seemed quite excited and was rapping on the window pane to speak to us.

"Hey Mum and Dad guess what?" She shrieked.

I wondered what this great news could be, hoping it would be another detox in a proper re-hab centre.

Wishful thinking on my part.

Louise quickly announced that she had been given a council flat and was being helped by her key workers to move in. They had arranged furniture through charities and all her benefits had been sorted out. Then she said "I will be going tomorrow as the flat is now vacant, and I can't wait."

With that news revealed she gave us a big smile and scooted off down the garden to her caravan and started to pile all her belongings into black bags.

It had been wonderful to see her so happy and excited. How different from the girl I had watched leaving the garden that morning, but then, not only had she had good news, she obviously had been able to get the drugs needed to make her feel good. To say that we were stunned was an understatement, every day seemed to bring another revelation. How many more surprises were in store for us?

We looked at one another and Ryan just shrugged his shoulders in disbelief.

Lou was given a lift by her key worker the next morning to her new flat in a nearby town and once again I began to clear up the mess left behind.

The caravan was in a poor state, the food that we had put in her cupboards had hardly been touched and evidence that had become so familiar had not been disposed of and was still everywhere to be seen.

Down the side of the bed was the tell-tale burnt silver paper and blackened marks were all over the table top. Well now she had gone from us again we both felt empty as the caravan she left behind that we so lovingly had prepared for her.

Holly worked in the same area that Louise had moved to so at least there was someone that could help her if needed.

Both Ryan and I were invited to see her when she had settled in and was surprised how spacious the flat was, and we once again filled the cupboards and got her extra furniture and appliances that she needed.

Lou seemed very excited and we felt a little better. Her key workers and social services were on her doorstep so we were confident that they were on the ball and would make sure Louise stayed on whatever her program was.

After a few weeks I arrived unannounced, there was still no sign of the boyfriend but Lou seemed very agitated. I had just popped in to drop some towels and extra bedding off to her and help her clean up what was becoming a grubby flat, when I thought I heard a noise in the cupboard, I tried to open the door but it seemed locked. the strange thing was there was no bolt or keyhole, I asked how to unlock it and Lou answered that it was stuck.

I then pulled hard on the door and the boyfriend fell out.

To say I was surprised was saying it mildly but I really saw the funny side of it as the embarrassed young man apologised saying Louise had insisted he hid from me.

I had to give in and accept that he was part of her life whether I liked it or not, and decided to just not worry about him anymore.

Both Lou and the boyfriend looked very thin and pale, Lou had developed spots and her teeth were looking yellow. Then I found needles under the mat, in the bed, in the corners behind the settee, I was in shock, but Louise had an answer for everything.

"It's not mine, we had someone stay and it was his." She explained.

Yes once again I believed her, I did not think that she could inject herself knowing how needle phobic she was, and it didn't dawn on me at the time that the boyfriend could be doing it.

At every opportunity I tried to look at her arms as she always kept them covered, even on the hottest summers day she would wear long sleeved jumpers. But she had become very clever at hiding any tell-tale marks she had on her body. When I was clearing out the endless rubbish that they seemed to constantly accrue, I found blood soaked swabs, and my heart sank. I could no longer justify giving her the benefit of the doubt as this was not helping me or her. I had to face it again, my daughter in my eyes was a hopeless junkie and until she really decided to quit this awful existence, she would continue to be an addict.

Louise had also started to become a nuisance for her sister at work, she would just turn up and ask for money or just want to see her.

Holly knew the security guard that worked in the building and he informed her that Lou had been spotted trying to shop lift in the area.

Her description had been sent out and she was being monitored by the police.

This really concerned Holly as she did not want to burdon us with anymore worries, so she decided to confront Lou the next time she appeared to try and make her understand that this was not the answer, as she would end up ruining her prospects for the future if she ended up in prison.

She didn't have to wait long as the next day a scruffy girl that was just recognisable as her sister appeared again.

Holly took her into her office and sat her down.

"Hallo Holly I just came in to ask if I could borrow ten pounds till next week?"

Holly had heard all this before and felt it was time to have a serious chat with Louise.

"No Lou I am not able to give you any more money, so do not ask me again. "She replied.

Lou seemed to just sit and stare at her.

Holly then told her about what would happen if she were caught shop lifting, and warned her that she was being watched.

"It will ruin your prospects Lou," Holly added.

Lou said nothing as Holly continued to give her sister some home truths, and before she knew it all the past frustrations and anger she felt about Louise's behaviour came flooding out.

Suddenly Louise began to cry, this was an emotion that Holly had not seen from her in a long time.

"It's no good crying Lou, its time you faced up to the fact that you need to get yourself help to get off this cycle of self-destructive behaviour."

Then falling to her knees, Louise blurted out something to Holly that made sense of all of the madness.

"When I was fourteen I was raped" she cried.

This stopped Holly in her tracks.

"No one believed me, and it hurt so much!" she was now trembling and blurting out the words as if they were burning her mouth.

Holly knew at once that Lou was telling the truth, and was horrified when hearing the terrible details of her sister's ordeal.

"I was fourteen and a virgin, and he took that away from me" she continued through the tears.

"I was bleeding and he didn't care, I was so frightened and there was no-one to help me!"

By now Holly was holding on to her young sister, not able to make it better and feeling so sorry that she had lived with this for so many years without being able to confide in her family.

"I had to numb the memory, I could not stand seeing his face every time I closed my eyes." she continued.

"I want to kill him for what he has done to me" sobbing uncontrollably Lou was distraught, but at the same time a weight was lifting from her shoulders and unbeknown to her, the healing process was beginning.

She had made a giant leap and Holly felt honoured that she had chosen her to be the one to confide in after so many years of torment.

She then told Holly of the events that led to her taking drugs.

This was to become the hardest thing to cope with for everyone.

I was yet to be told.

# Chapter 12

## IT ALL MADE SENSE

$\mathcal{J}$ was sitting in the garden trying imagine what it would be like if everything was back normal, although I was now not sure what normal was. There had been more regular trips to my parent's house, to help my mother with Dads on going health problems. We had been travelling back and forth for endless hospital appointments as my father was by now not well enough to go anywhere alone as he was very unstable on his feet.

When we saw the specialist and asked about Dads progress we were told that the results of his treatment were as they expected, and they did not elaborate any further. When asked if he had any questions, my dearest Dad said no.

I knew that they were only giving him the information they thought he could cope with, and my father did not want to hear any more bad news.

Although very worrying it was helping me to keep my mind off Louise and her problems, and it was an opportunity to spend quality time with my parents.

The sun went in and mindful that Ryan would be home soon, I came in to start dinner, when Holly arrived looking worried.

"Hi Mum" she said in a quiet voice.

Instantly my instincts kicked in, there was something wrong, what now I thought.

"Can I have a chat Mum?" This question was only going to have one answer from me.

"Of course Holly what is the matter?"

I asked dreading the answer.

"Mum I had Louise in the office today and she was in a bit of a state"

Oh, here we go again I thought she needs money.

We sat in the kitchen and Holly began to explain what she had been told.

I was informed that Louise walked into the office looking terrible and Holly having had enough of her untimely visits told her off for thinking she could come in whenever she liked. She omitted telling me about the shop lifting and police, but added that she had off loaded all the anger she had been storing to try and make Louise understand what an impact she had on all of her family's lives.

Then as gently as she could Holly told me that Louise had confessed that she had been raped at the age of fourteen, and none of her friends had believed her!

The words hardly out of her mouth, Holly began to become tearful and found it difficult to carry on.

I was struck dumb, not being able to comprehend what I was being told.

This surely could not have happened to my beautiful daughter, as we had always tried to make sure she was taken and brought home when going out.

"Where did this happen?" I managed to speak although I was confused, and in shock

Holly answered "When she went to one of the discos."

As this was being revealed to me I thought back to the weekend when Louise was fourteen.

It was the last time she had stayed the night over with her friend Sammi.

Holly continued to tell me that they had gone to the local disco and had met up with some boys. Lou had not met them before and they were slightly older, but Sammi seemed to be very familiar with one of them and had begun flirting almost immediately. Louise and her friend had spent most of the evening with these boys, when Louise was asked by her friend if she would go and buy get some cigarettes. Another vice that I had not realised she had.

One of the boys offered to go with her to the off licence to get some.

I could understand that as I was about her age when I had started smoking.

We all did things that we were not supposed to when we were young.

I can remember wanting to go to the pictures desperate to see Whatever Happened to Baby Jane, but I was not old enough as it was X rated and you had to be over 18 to get in. After putting on makeup and my friend's stiletto heels I managed to pass and got to see the film.

With this in mind I could quite understand Louise's behaviour, but ultimately she had put herself in a vulnerable situation, and being innocent was unaware that danger could be around the corner. As they walked in the darkness Louise had felt comfortable with this boy, at her age she thought she knew everything, she did not pick up any sign that she was about to be attacked.

As they entered an alley he suddenly pounced on her and brutally raped her, she was so frightened that was not able even to scream, she was also a virgin so had no idea what was happening until he forced himself on her. When the deed was over he calmly got up and walked back to the disco leaving Louise to try and pull herself together and get back to her friend.

On entering the venue her friend asked were the cigarettes were and Louise blurted out what had happened. To her surprise her friend said she didn't believe her and said she was making it up. The boy had returned to the disco as if nothing had happened and was busy chatting to another girl.

"Mum, Lou was beside herself with fear and just had no idea what to do next.

The thought of phoning the police was just as scary, she thought that they would not believe her either."

I was finding it hard to take in what I was being told.

As Holly continued I became very angry, Lou always seemed to be at the mercy of so called friends and this betrayal by Sammi left me reeling.

"She wanted to come home but her friend was more concerned that her parents would make a fuss, as they were underage and had to be over sixteen to enter the venue Sammi had made Louise promise to say nothing."

In Louise's eyes if her friend did not believe her, we would not either.

The rest of the evening was spent with Louise in the toilets trying to clean up while her friend continued to socialise. By the time they were picked up Lou was ready to just come home and set about trying to get that night over so she could get home as quickly as possible, and Sammi having been very distant to her, sat in the car gushing to her mother about the great time they had.

Another reason she felt she could not tell us was that she would have to somehow prove in court that she had been raped by this person, and there had been no witnesses, and the thought of having to face him in a courtroom was unthinkable for her.

I began to remember how quiet and withdrawn she had been when she returned from that last sleep over.

Why I had not been there for her, why had I not taken enough notice of her?

I would have moved heaven and earth to make sure this evil boy was brought to justice. How isolated she must have felt, and through her tears Holly then told me how Louise had then gone to school the following morning only to be taunted by her other so called friends, being called a tart, and slapper, all the usual bullying name calling that goes with teenage girls. Yes her so called best friend had told everyone that Louise had ruined the night by making out she had been raped when she had volunteered to go outside with this boy. After that, every day became more difficult for her as wherever she went there were whispers and sniggering from her peers.

She would normally sit alone in the playground watching the rest of her classmates enjoying themselves, while she was excluded making her feel very alone, so her only choice was to withdraw from their company.

It was at this time that she had started to bully her brother, and at that point it all seemed to make sense as things were beginning to add up in my mind.

Sammi however had omitted telling them that she was the person that had asked Lou to get some cigarettes, but after all she was fourteen too and her priorities were that of a child not an adult.

My heart sank, I can remember back I wondering why the weekend sleep overs had suddenly stopped and Louise was not mixing with her friends anymore.

Again we had put that down to teenage behaviour, and the normal falling out with friends. Then the boyfriend had appeared on the scene so Louise had seemed preoccupied with him.

Holly's words were becoming a mist in my head, I just felt nauseous and so very sad that my child had this terrible crime happen to her and we had not been able to stop it or help her come to terms with it.

I had no answers, no idea what to do now, this was new ground for us and I was just not equipped to know what to do.

"Mum the worst is yet to come" Holly took a deep breath.

"She got her first fix from outside the school gates."

Holly explained that the drug dealers would stand near to the gates and offer free drugs to the children. Louise had been so traumatised that she tried drugs to get the horrible memory from her brain as she was experiencing flash backs, feeling guilty, isolated, frightened, and ostracised from her friends.

She had told Holly that every time she closed her eyes she would see his face bearing down on her, and could not get the smell of him out of her mind.

The more she had fought him the more he hurt her as he seemed to get stronger.

She blamed herself for getting into that situation, but at the same time could not understand why he had done this to her as he had seemed to be a nice person.

When she had finally managed to get back to the disco he was acting as if nothing had happened and she was left desolate after her friends reaction to her plight. It had all become too much for her to bear so her only thoughts were to numb the pain.

This is what the drug dealers look for, they seek out vulnerable children give them free drugs and get them hooked, then they start to charge money for their supplies. Louise had started her downward decline by smoking pot, and the odd taking amphetamines, usually mixing them with alcohol.

By the time Louise left school she was well on the road to becoming an addict, and when we had taken her on holiday to Greece she went through a bad time as she had to go a week without any drugs, therefore the mood swings and anti-social behaviour could have partially been because she was withdrawing from her regular supply of drugs.

The terrible memories came flooding back, I could not even cry, all I wanted to do was see Louise and hold her close to me and tell her that I loved her and that with the right help she would get over this.

In my view that evil boy was still raping my daughter as she had suffered so much pain since that awful night.

If only we could turn the clock back, the thought of my innocent daughter being violated in such a brutal way was beyond my comprehension, was there anything we should have done differently? I asked myself. These thoughts were going round and round, and once again I felt guilty. It was too late to inform the police now as it was unthinkable to expect Lou to be able to be strong enough to confront this man and cope with what she was already going through.

So I decided to give her time and talk it through with us.

James had seen Holly's car in the drive and decided to pop in just as we had finished talking. He came bouncing in and suddenly stopped in his tracks when he saw the despair on our faces. Holly had already made arrangements to have him over to her place at the weekend to give him a break from the continual worry of his sisters addiction, but this would be brought forward as he would have to be told and I was not able to do the deed this time.

Holly took him upstairs and gave him the news, and after being given the outline not the details, to my relief he packed his bags and decided to leave with Holly to stay with her for a while. We hugged each other as he left, and red eyed, he promised me that he would be ok, and was looking forward to spending time with his sister and Paul.

Holly then said she would tell Emma for me, and I was relieved that she was taking the responsibility from my shoulders.

This left me the unenviable task of informing her father and he would soon be arriving home. The house was very still after everyone had gone, I was thinking of Louise and trying to imagine how she must have been feeling, and how scared she must have been when she was being violated. All those years of holding this terrible burden inside, not knowing how to tell us. How I was going to tell her father was beyond me. I braced myself for a long talk with him and decided we would have to go and see Lou the next morning.

# Chapter 13

---

## A DANGEROUS PLACE

*R*yan and I had a very intense evening I did not know the best way to break the news to him so just said the words. He was, like me, in total shock when hearing the word rape. His first reaction was anger and frustration over it all, he wanted to find him and kill him. Then as it sunk in, the realisation of it all and his inability to have prevented this crime from happening to her came to the fore, and we both wept together.

After another sleepless night with Ryan, discussing what to do next, I rang her in the morning to make arrangements to go and see her.

We both wanted to be there together, as it was important that Lou saw we were united in our belief of her story, and this was one occasion where Ryan was not prepared to come home from work, and spend all night talking, for this had been a mind blowing moment for us all.

We arrived just as the boyfriend was putting out the rubbish he nodded to us which meant hello.

When Lou opened the door we could see she was worried and looked very pensive and I suspected she had also been up all night worried about our reaction. Both Ryan and I grabbed hold of her and just held her close.

The emotion that we were all feeling was very intense and words at that time seemed unimportant as we knew instinctively that Lou was finally crossing over to the other side and we were confident that the process of healing would now begin in earnest.

She began to tell us what had happened in her own words.

There were no details of the actual attack, as it was still very difficult for her to speak us about it but I felt that for the first time in a long time we were actually getting somewhere and she was finally opening up to us. She told us that her counsellors had known about her rape and had tried to help her come to terms with it and in all fairness to them had tried to encourage Lou to tell us and trust that she would be ok. I was a little hurt that she had been unable to confide in us, but at the same time understood that she was feeling very vulnerable and after all the recent events, had not known how to get started.

We asked if she was getting any help with coming to terms with this crime from her key workers, and whether she had thought about contacting the rape crisis helpline. We were assured that she was to have counselling arranged through her doctor, but it was for six sessions only. The powers that be had decided that this is adequate for anyone needing counselling for whatever reason.

Once again I was not surprised at the lack of understanding from the professionals. It seemed to always be about ticking boxes, forgetting the obvious, as we are all individuals. As we talked, Lou began to look a lot calmer, and admitted she felt so much better for telling us because she really did not think we would believe her. Although we were still reeling from the whole scenario, both Ryan and I made sure she understood that we both believed her, and told her that whatever she wanted to do about it, we would be ok with her decision.

My reaction was to find this beast and bring him to justice, as in my view until Lou had come completely through her addiction he was still raping my daughter.

"I am not strong enough to deal with him yet, so for the time being I am keeping it at the back of my mind." she said. In one way I was agreeing with her, but knew she had not really confronted her feelings about the attack, and this would not help with her recovery.

The boyfriend was present at our meeting and did not have a lot to say, but I didn't want to talk to him anyway as he was clearly showing signs of drug use. He did mention however that he had not known about the attack until Louise had confessed to him the night before, so maybe he was in shock too.

Both Ryan and I sat most of the day with Lou, her father wanting to find this young man and prosecute him but at the same time being mindful that Louise was the only one that could make that decision. I could not even begin to imagine how she had managed to live with this for so long.

As the day drew on we started talking about her feelings and how she was trying to get her dose of methadone reduced in order to start another detox programme. We sat and listened interrupting only to tell her that we were behind her and that we were sure she would be able to beat this. To have spent all day with her was something that had not happened for a long time. As we were leaving we both noticed the flat was becoming very squalid, and all the other tenants were either drug addicts or alcoholics.

On many occasions I had seen needles in the hall well and the windows of the ground floor flats were constantly being smashed. There were many fights and threats from various unsavoury characters that would turn up at all hours of the day. Across the hall Lou's neighbour had been an alcoholic for many years and was always entertaining men at all hours of the night. For once we were glad she had the boyfriend with her as it was becoming worse.

We were not happy with Louise living there but she would not come home without the boyfriend being on tow, and we were still not convinced that both of them would stick to their prescription without going to the dealers for extra drugs, and that was unacceptable for us.

Then one evening we had a call from the boyfriend, there had been a fire in the building and their flat had been broken into, also I discovered there was no fire escape on her landing, and she lived on the top floor, so it was pure luck that Louise and the boyfriend had been out when it happened. We rushed round and it was chaos, the people next door had some fellow alcoholics round and one had set the next door alight. This was truly getting out of hand and I could not bear the thought of her living in such awful conditions any longer.

We had no choice but to have them both stay with us while we tried to make good the flat again and this was going to take a while. In the meantime I wrote to the housing officers stating my worry at the lack of an adequate fire escape.

I also mentioned our concerns that she was living in a volatile situation, and knowing her past, we were surprised that they had housed her there.

Her councillors did the same, and for once both the professionals and I were singing from the same hymn sheet.

My son stayed out more and more when they moved in, still not being able to talk to us about his sister, and I was continuing to go back and forth to my parents house helping my mother to look after Dad. We tried to settle into as normal an existence as we could, avoiding the boyfriend as much as possible. Every day they would disappear for hours, I thought it was because they wanted to be out of the house as it was strained to say the least.

I was wrong on that score as I was to find out later, they were spending most of each day waiting for the drug dealers to arrive with their heroin.

The thing about these pushers is that they have the trump card, and turn up when they deem fit, by the time the poor user has been waiting, they become desperate and are more likely to buy more.

They never have enough money so it is put down as a loan, and then they are reeled in, and it's constant. We had already been down that road and had hoped we would never have to go there again.

Then something very strange happened, Louise came downstairs one evening and sat looking at me, not saying a word but I knew that something was on her mind. "Mum, Lou began, I want to talk to you"

Ryan was out so I assumed there was to be another revelation.

Well there was but it was not what I expected.

"It's about Gary," yes this was the boyfriends name.

I had been unable to bring myself to call him by his name before as I had no intention of recognising him as human being.

"Well?" I answered deciding to keep it short.

"I want to tell you about him and what he has had to put up with in his life" Louise replied ignoring the fact I had a face like thunder.

I can remember thinking, this had better be good.

Louise went on to tell me how he had come from a large family with four brothers his mother had left them when he was eight and the children were left to be brought up by his alcoholic father. His Dad had tried his best to look after them all and keep them together, but through his father's addiction, life had not always been easy.

Gary had on many occasions had to walk the streets to avoid being attacked by his drunken father when he was binging.

He dreaded Christmas as his father would celebrate with his uncles and the drink would flow freely.

On Christmas day, knowing he would be beaten if he showed his face while his Dad was awake, he would wander around until he felt it was safe to sneak back indoors.

The more she told me the more I understood that this boy had been subject to a violent home life and a mother that rejected him.

As Gary had grown up he had clearly been damaged by his dysfunctional upbringing, and because of his low self-esteem played truant from school, the consequences of that being, he was expelled.

He had left school not finishing his education so had no formal qualifications to help him get a good job.

He had started to smoke pot at an early age just to get through the day.

His brothers also bullied him although he was the eldest, they treated him as the weakest among them.

Louise had even witnessed his father hitting him for no reason and pushing him down the stairs, but through all this he desperately loved his family and wanted to have a good relationship with his father.

The one person that he could rely on was his grandfather, he had shielded Gary from a lot of the violence and they were very close.

Unfortunately for him his grandfather died around the time he was expelled so his mentor and advocate was lost to him and thinking he had no-one to turn to with his troubles found solace by taking drugs.

I felt myself well up with anger at the thought of what he had been through, and I felt ashamed that I had judged him so harshly.

I had been so convinced that it was his fault that Louise was using drugs that I was blind to the fact that maybe there might be a reason he took drugs too and that he was as much a victim as Lou and not the enemy I had hated for so long.

I then began to understand how much they both relied on each other.

They had supported each other with all the terrible things they had witnessed and been through. Gary did not make any demands on Louise and had tried on numerous occasions get help to come off the drugs but had no support from his family.

I felt myself sink back into the sofa as more awful stories came to light.

I had been for so long blaming everyone else for the horror that we were going through. I had done exactly what I had accused the professionals of doing, and treated Gary not as an individual but as a manipulative stereotype drug user.

I was guilty of treating him with contempt without actually taking the time and effort to find out about his problems. I was very humbled by my own misunderstanding of it all.

I was again in a situation that I didn't want to be in.

I wanted to weep for the lost childhood of this boy, but also wanted to shake him for allowing himself to be in the same position as Louise.

We talked for an age and when she finally finished, I told her that I would begin to try and understand him more and that I was sorry that I had judged him so harshly. By now Lou and

I were exhausted and I sent her to bed while I sat alone going over what I had been told, as I would now have to tell her father when he came home. This was beginning to have a pattern.

Poor Ryan, every time he walked through the door another drama seemed to greet him. We had long forgotten the usual honey I'm home call as he entered the house. Now he would peep round the door to see if the coast was clear, and by looking at my face would automatically know that once again I had something to tell him.

Tonight was no exception. so all he asked was, "how long is it going to take?"

Well this was going to be a long conversation, especially as he had felt the same about Gary and unfortunately treated him with the same contempt as I had.

# *Chapter 14*

## THE MOVE

*T*he next morning Ryan just managed to get up to go to work as the conversation the night before had been, as expected intense and long.

We were both tired and fed up with not knowing what was next when the phone rang. The council had offered Louise a ground floor one bedroomed flat in another area. I was amazed that they had come up with a better place for her and we made plans to help them move.

Once again furniture was bought, food put into the cupboards and both Holly and Emma helped to clean the flat for them. Holly and Emma after all the revelations had become understanding of Louise's problem, and were beginning to come to terms with it all rallying round to help and support her.

James as usual kept his distance as he really found it tough to accept that she was still not clean, but he was young and as far as he was concerned it was black or white no in between. Many hands make light work, Holly and Paul cleaned the kitchen cupboards, Emma painted the lounge, Ryan and Gary put up the curtain rails, without arguing, and I followed behind tidying up after everyone else. Lou on the other hand seemed to just walk around doing nothing.

In the meantime I made a real effort with Gary and started to try and talk to him. He was a bit hesitant at first and could not look me in the eye but we were beginning to build bridges. Louise and Gary both still on methadone had started reducing their dose slowly, and were on the waiting list to get clean so we all had high hopes. The flat was in a nice quiet area and I was more relaxed for the first time in ages. I then left it to them to make what arrangements they needed to get help for another detox.

This left me able to concentrate on my father as he was deteriorating.

When I look back he was so brave, he never complained and always asked how Louise was. Life was jogging along when suddenly my father became very unwell and was hospitalised. The young doctor came into the cubical and Mum and I sat at the end of the bed expecting him to be admitted for observation.

Well we were wrong on that score. The actual words this young doctor used were.

"Frank, do you want to keep coming into hospital, or would you like to go home as we cannot do any more for you?"

The words kept echoing round my head, was he telling my Dad what I thought he was telling him?

Mum and I looked at each other with dread, we were hearing a doctor giving Dad a choice of places to end his days.

"Or there is a hospice if you prefer." He added, not giving either Mum or me eye contact.

Dad looked at him and asked

"Will I make it to my 80th birthday?"

"When is it?" he enquired

"Three weeks." Dad replied.

After a short pause the young doctor put his hand on my father's arm and said quietly to him.

"I cannot be sure" Dad looked at me and then at his wife and gave a slight smile. The silence in the room was only broken by the gentle sobs of my mother.

"Well I had better drive you home then Dad," I said.

With that statement my father turned to me and asked how they would be able to cope. In that instant I realised there was no other option but for me to move in with them and help my mother care for her husband, and I would have the privilege of helping her.

"No problem Dad I can stay with you and Mum and I we can easily look after you between us" I announced. With that said, the doctor made a hasty retreat to discharge my father, leaving us trying to come to terms with the news we had just been given. Louise and her troubles were now on the back burner as I had other things to deal with.

When I arrived home I asked my husband if it would be allright if I were to move in with my parents to help mum with the everyday care of my father.

Immediately he said that it would be no problem at all and held me close saying how much he loved me. Through all the trials and tribulations that we had faced together, our love for each other had never wavered, even when we were both at our lowest, we knew we remain strong and always be together.

We arranged for my sisters to come and stay at my house so that they could visit and spend time with Mum and Dad, while I remained with my parents and helped with the everyday care of a very sick man.

Ryan was coping as best he could and I managed to go home for a couple of hours every day to catch up on housework and just have a break.

It was so nice to have my sisters there too as dad did not want to be left alone, so it gave me a chance to recharge my batteries and return to my home and catch up with Ryan and whoever was popping in at the time.

Holly and Paul spent many evenings with Ryan to give him support, and Emma and the boys popped in on a regular basis.

James had started to go out with his father on occasion so the family seemed to be closer than ever before.

After Louise and Gary had been round to stay one day, I noticed blood on the sheets on the bed where they had been sleeping. I thought Louise had an accident so changed the bedding not feeling the need to mention it for fear of embarrassing her. Then every time they visited and I came home to see them for a couple of hours I kept finding these random blood splashes in the bathroom.

At first I dismissed them as I was sure that there would be an innocent reason why this was happening.

My sisters had moved back to their homes after spending Dads birthday with him. They had wanted to stay longer but work and family commitments had not allowed it, but they were happy in the knowledge that they had both said what they wanted to say to their father, so they left the next day, and Mum and I continued with the daily routine of looking after him. Dad was now on oxygen and had stopped eating very much. This worried Mum as she was still trying to cure him. It was very difficult to accept that he was really going to leave us.

He was getting weaker now, but was pretty smug at beating the three week deadline that he had been given by the doctor. This birthday would be his last one and I was overcome with sadness.

Every year I would search the shops for the most silliest present I could find for him as he loved having a good laugh. He had a large box stored in the garage full of noisy toys that he had been given over the years, his favourite being Bertie Bass the singing fish. He was even more proud of it as apparently the Queen had been given one.

"What's good enough for Liz is good enough for me." he often joked.

I remember it held pride of place above the hall table and would start singing as soon as anyone walked by.

Needless to say it was not there for long as it drove Mum mad, and as Dad would not throw any of his stuff away, ended up where all the other irritating gifts ended up, in the ever expanding storage box.

This year had been different I had been unable to get out to buy anything, but Dad did not seem to mind, and he was so weak now he could not even summon the strength to laugh.

My father started to hold court for the never ending flow of family members wanting to see him. This was a welcome distraction for him even though he was tired most of the time, there was nothing he enjoyed more than giving advice whether it was wanted or not. This included Louise when she finally came to see him. He did not judge her, but said she needed to get herself well and she promised him she would. I could see that she was greatly affected by seeing how frail her grandad had become, even more than had I realised at the time.

He gave personal belongings to members of the family and kept as cheerful as he could even when it was becoming difficult. Then one morning after a particularly bad night he said I have had enough I just want to sleep. Mum and

I had been giving him his medication to open his airways but breathing was beginning to be a real struggle for him.

I rang the doctor and was instructed to increase his dose of medication and just try keeping him comfortable. I knew that it was just a matter of time before I lost my dear father, and the thought of that was unbearable.

Mum was on auto pilot, still not giving up, puffing up his pillows and constantly trying to encourage him to eat. That evening dads breathing became more laboured and there were longer pauses between each breath. He had not been conscious for most of the day and he seemed to be showing signs of shutting down, so decided to leave mum and dad together and went to bed.

Dad passed away that evening, very peacefully with mum at his side.

Our rock had left us, this strong kind loving man was missed already and would always be missed by everyone who knew him.

The events of the next week became a blur to me.

My sisters were informed, and they immediately returned to help with the funeral arrangements. I moved back home to Ryan, relieved that I was home but feeling guilty for being relieved. I could not stop crying, I think that the grief I had encountered with Louise and now the loss of Dad suddenly hit me again and I was in meltdown.

I was not functioning well and felt that I could not cope with any more sadness.

My sisters took over and Ryan did all the necessary paper work for Mum.

I spent most of my time wandering about the house, going over again and again in my mind, the last few days I spent with my father.

He had not been the type of man to show his feelings, but one evening when Mum was in the kitchen I took his hand and told him how much I loved him and that I was so lucky to have had such a wonderful father. He turned to me and with a smile, managed to give my hand a squeeze and whispered that he loved me too, and said I will always be his little girl. How strange I thought, that he would use those words, as that is how I felt when I looked at my children especially Louise. I had not realised that my parents still saw me as a child.

The day of the funeral arrived and Ryan decided to take Louise and Gary in his car. I was already with mum and my sisters at her house helping with the last minute preparations.

Mum was being very brave, but I confess I was useless, and just kept breaking down. As friends and family arrived I was getting anxious as Ryan was never late but time was running out and there was no sign of him. Finally I saw a familiar face and gave a sigh of relief.

He took me to one side and explained the reason he was later than he wanted to be. Louise had turned up wearing scruffy trainers and looking very dirty.

Gary was in old smelly jeans with holes in. He felt he had no choice and rushed to the town to get something for them to wear as they were totally inappropriately dressed for a funeral.

As I looked out into the garden where they were having a cigarette I noticed that Louise was sweating and looked very strange, and Gary was shifting backwards and forwards unable to keep still.

This was my Father's funeral and were both seemingly worse for wear on drugs.

Louise was visibly in distress, in my view not with the loss of her Grandfather I thought but because she needed heroin. The ceremony over we all arrived back to Mums home for the wake. Lou was getting more agitated and said that she had to leave, I knew why and told them both to go. Some of the other guests commented how much weight she had lost and enquired whether she was ill.

Ryan stepped in and assured them she was fine but was just getting over the flu.

Then the final straw came and hit us hard.

Holly and Paul took me to one side and told me that before the funeral Gary had been in our bathroom for a long time. Paul had arrived early and started to get ready for the funeral as he and Holly were staying the night with us. After seeing Lou and Gary and what a mess they were both in, he was suspicious that things were not right again. He overheard that Ryan was taking them into town to get some clothes so took the opportunity to investigate and had sneaked a look in Louise's overnight bag while she was downstairs.

He told me he had been shocked to find syringes and swabs hidden in a small box at the bottom of the rucksack, so knew why Gary had spent so much time in the toilet.

I began to realise now why I had been finding blood stains splashed up the walls in my bathroom. Losing my Dad and going through the same thing over and over again with my daughter had now really begun to get to me.

How many more times would I have to listen to feeble excuses and blatant lies?

How many more promises of detoxes? how many more times would we have our hopes raised only to have them dashed? No more I thought, I can't go through this anymore. I did not know how Ryan would feel and knew we would be having another of our late night discussions, but I had come to the end and felt I could not watch this anymore.

I suddenly became very determined to stop this once and for all, but it would be after the funeral when I had time to talk to my husband as we had to decide together what the best action would be.

# Chapter 15

## I WALK AWAY

**W**e arrived home and I managed to wait until the next morning to speak to Ryan about the finding of needles by Paul. Everyone left early in the morning so we were alone and able to talk. I told him that I could not cope with this anymore and that I felt we were not helping Louise by giving her money, and helping with bills as Ryan had been paying for her electric and gas. I told him that I needed to walk away in order for her to realise that she had no choice but to seriously get clean. I was surprised but relieved at his response, he had been thinking the same as we both knew that we could not save her, she had to do that herself.

This was not an easy decision to reach but we both agreed that it would ultimately be the best for all. Lou was now turning twenty and had been going through this now for nearly six years, we had never stopped loving her and we felt miserable that it was coming to this. We decided that we would give ourselves time to really think about it and we decided to wait for a few weeks.

My mother was coping as best she could, and I was trying to spend as much time with her as possible.

My parents had been married for sixty years, and Mum could not imagine being without her husband as they were truly soul mates. Like my mother I was finding it difficult to adjust to a different life. It was not just the fact that he had died, but the everyday care was missed too. My mother had gone from a very busy life, running a home, going with Dad on all his hospital appointments, dealing with all the normal everyday problems that occur, and being a full time carer, to suddenly being alone in her bungalow. I had to put my grief on a back burner because it was time for me to confront Louise.

I had not seen her very much since the funeral and both Ryan and I agreed that it would be the best option to walk away and pray that it shocked her into getting clean once and for all. We both knew it would be a big gamble as she could easily go the other way and drift deeper into her addiction. We had also offered her private counselling for her rape, but she was in no frame of mind to take us up on our offer. I rang Emma and asked her to come round with me to see Louise and Gary. I explained that we had decided to cut all ties with her as we was not prepared to continue anymore with this hell on earth.

Since the death of my father I had begun to look at my life through a different angle, and had realised that I needed to trust in my instincts and let fate decide the outcome for Louise.

Through all the years of dealing with Lou's problems, I had neglected my home life with my husband and felt it was time to try and return to some kind of normality. It had been clear to me for a long time that we were not in control of the situation and we could not cure our daughter. I also had to take into consideration my other children who had witnessed so much despair from us and give them some time to heal too. I was abandoning my daughter again but it was for the best reason I hoped, as we seemed to have made so many mistakes in all of this I just prayed this time we were truly doing what was best for all.

Emma said she would come and take Gary away for a couple of hours while I talked to Louise.

The journey there was very hard, both Emma and I were silent, as there was nothing that either could say that would with help the situation.

Ryan knew of my intent and backed me one hundred per cent.

We arrived just as Louise had got up. She looked tired and flushed, her eyes were drooping and

I noticed that once again one eye was blinking independently of the other.

There was a musky smell in the flat mixed with cigarette smoke and on the coffee table there were many black marks and burns.

"Hi Lou," I said, and ignoring the debris on the floor made my way over to a chair opposite her. After Emma greeted her she explained that she was going to take Gary out for a while so that we could talk. With that said, Emma beckoned to Gary who was leaning on the sofa with a vacant look on his face, to follow her outside.

As they left Emma caught my eye, we both knew that this was the start of my withdrawal and we both were afraid for all of us.

I sat on the chair moving a half-eaten pizza, and Louise sat opposite, her gaze fixed on the floor. After a moment I decided to speak, and once I started, like Holly, I found all the years of worry, upset, anger and frustration starting to pour out of me.

"Louise" I began, "have you any idea what you did at your Grandfathers funeral?"

No response.

"You showed total disrespect for him and all the family, both you and Gary turned up the worse for wear.

You had not even made an effort to at least wear something appropriate.

Your father had to drive you to town and get some suitable clothing, making him late!" I continued, "and all you seemed interested in was getting it over so you could get your next fix."

No response.

By now I was in overdrive and nothing was going to stop the flow.

"I had to watch my father fight for his life while you seem to be determined to destroy yours."

Louise by now was trying to speak, but I was not interested in anything she may have had to say at that moment in time. Then the crunch came and I used my trump card.

"You promised your grandfather you would make the effort and get well, how do you think he would feel knowing you had broken your word?"

I then recognised a flash of emotion from her but was blinded by my own determination to get out all the anger I was feeling.

"Do you know what you are?" I asked.

As I spoke I fixed my gaze on her and for once she looked me in the eye, a cold empty stare that I interpreted as defiance, but was later to learn that she was desperately broken hearted over his death and had simply taken more heroin to deaden the pain.

This whole scenario had not been just about taking drugs to feed her addiction, but more to the point she had used to try and take away the pain of her loss.

I had not for one moment considered this, as I had been so wrapped up in my own grief, but I should have known better than to judge her without thinking.

So I blindly carried on going over all the past while Louise just sat and looked down.

"You are a druggie, your disgusting, you're living in squalor and this is your choice." My voice was getting louder, and I surprised myself at the way I was speaking to her.

As the venom poured out of me I noticed that Louise was showing no response at all, and I thought it was just words to her. Then I suppose the whole reason that drug users take drugs in the first place is to numb all feelings, well it was working as far as I could see.

My rant lasted for about an hour only pausing for the odd break down and tears from me. Louise on the other hand just sat there with a look of despair on her face. It was awful, and I hoped that I was getting through to that little girl that was locked away from me, "Well Louise," by now I was tired and worn out by it all, having got everything off my chest I had one last statement to add.

"I am not prepared to watch you kill yourself and I did not bring you into this world to watch you destroy your life, so I am not going to see you or speak to you until you are clean or can prove to me that you are making an effort."

With that statement I hoped something would now click with her but again she just sat there looking at me.

Emma arrived back with Gary and I got up to leave.

Louise was now looking shocked but was still not speaking, she had heard all this before, but at least she would not be sleeping in a public toilet this time.

I said goodbye and there was no hug or kiss, she just stared at me as I walked out the door. The coldness of her stare brought dread to my heart, had I condemned her to this for the rest of her life? Had I done the right thing?

Would this stop the drug abuse, or would we get a phone call saying she had overdosed and was in hospital or worse that we had lost her?

These questions were going round in my mind, but the decision we had made we felt had to be right for all the family, and that was what it was all about in the end.

We could have taken her in again but she would have continued to use drugs whether she was at home or away, so at least I did not have to watch it anymore, and on the journey home both Emma and I went over what had happened, trying to convince ourselves that Louise, my beautiful daughter would come through.

We were not giving up on her, we never would, but we had run out of ideas.

When we arrived home James Holly and Ryan were there and we all sat round the table going over the last six years and trying to convince ourselves that we would all come through this in the end.

# *Chapter 16*

## CALM

It was early autumn and it had been two months since I had spoken to Louise.

We had no idea what she was doing, and we felt it best not to try and find out.

Ryan and I were much better and decided to go on holiday on with Mum to escape and recharge our batteries.

We had decided to go to Mallorca for a week and catch the last of the warm weather. It was so lovely to spend time away and not have any worries.

Mum still grieving, was in her element as she was for a short time able to forget the loneliness she was experiencing since dads death. She decided that it would be her job to cook, and in her eyes, I reverted back to being her child.

I happily obliged as it gave her purpose and there is nothing like my mother's cooking.

We were nearing the end of the holiday when I suddenly felt very unwell.

I had a sharp pain in my back and having had a prolapsed disc years ago assumed I had either pulled a muscle or prolapsed again.

I had always got a stock of anti-inflammatory pills with me and proceeded to take them. They had no effect and the pain was so intense I collapsed onto the bed unable to relieve the discomfort.

Needless to say the doctor was called and through his broken English we understood that he was admitting me to the local hospital.

Convinced this was a fuss about nothing I was not happy about it but agreed on Ryan's insistence. The ambulance arrived and I was bundled in with mum and Ryan on tow. After having many tests including a scan I was diagnosed with having gall stones, and apparently one had travelled to my liver and blocked a duct thus causing the acute pain.

Well I was dumbfounded at the results, I had no idea that this was the cause and after medication I was sent on my way to get treatment when I returned home.

Everyone was convinced that the years of stress had been a factor for my collapse, and this made me more determined to try and relax and calm down.

James was a lot happier and we had taken him out on a few occasions.

He was now able to talk about his feelings a bit more and it was nice to hear him whistling and being generally a lot happier.

Louise was no longer part of our everyday conversation and it was really a relief to not have to face her. Laughter began to return to our household, and plans were being made for the coming Christmas celebrations. I always had the family round for Boxing day and this year was going to be no exception, although a bit different, as Dad and Louise would not be there.

Mum said she would be at home, as my sister was coming to spend it with her, but they would both come over for Boxing Day.

I could not remember the last time we had such a beautiful autumn, the leaves were very vibrant and living in the country meant we were spoilt for views of woodlands with they're brightly coloured canopies. The nights were drawing in and the crisp mornings told us that winter and Christmas were fast approaching.

I had decided to go shopping for gifts.

The stores in the town had started to decorate their windows with all manner of Christmas decorations, and the familiar sound of popular Christmas tunes including Slades classic, "Here it is merry Christmas" filled each shop.

As I looked around I kept seeing things that I knew Louise would love.

Try as I might to concentrate on Ryan's gift, I kept looking at clothes that she would wear, jewellery that would look so pretty on her, and handbags.

Every birthday we had got her a new handbag as she loved them so much, the funkier the better.

It was as if every time I turned my head another item would catch my eye.

"Stop this," I scolded myself, but it was no use, I felt the tears welling up and made a hasty retreat to the nearest changing room to try and compose myself.

Why was I feeling like this? it was just too much to bear and I returned home empty handed and feeling very alone.

As I sat in the kitchen going over the day's events and still being puzzled at my reaction, it dawned on me that although Lou had not been part of my life for a while, I had not stopped thinking about her and wanted so desperately to include her in our family celebrations. At the same time I was still angry with her, and not ready to see her.

I was in a quandary, surely if she was off drugs we would have heard by now, but she had not made any contact either, and was probably still very hurt over my harsh words. Oh how I regretted that decision now, I felt guilty and cross with myself for being so sure we were right all the time, when in fact we may have been wrong again. I was unable to find a solution as I had no news from her and did not know how she was doing.

Oh why had I asked the impossible? thus condemning myself to never seeing my beautiful daughter again. I had by now convinced myself that I had done the wrong thing in walking away. Since I walked away every phone call had been a worry for me because it could have been the police giving me the news that I had always dreaded.

Ryan arrived home just as I had dried my eyes, and immediately asked why I had been crying. I confessed to my feelings and after some thought, Ryan came up with the right answer for me.

"Get her the clothes and gifts that you want her to have and I will take them round to her, and fill a box with food to last her a couple of weeks, then we can be assured she is not going without, and I can take the opportunity to see how she is" He replied.

Once again he came up with the right answer. I knew that I could always rely on him to support me and at the same time he could make sure his daughter was ok. Without further ado I was out the door back to the high street buying all the gifts I had seen for her.

That evening was spent wrapping her presents and sorting out the food parcel.

Ryan then said he would call to let her know he would be round with her gifts.

While he was dialling her number I fussed around the pile of gifts, which had included some for Gary too.

Louise answered the phone and spoke to her father as if nothing had happened.

"Hi Dad," she said

"Hi Lou," was the reply

I tried not to listen in to the conversation and Ryan kept it matter of fact.

"I am in your area next week and have some Christmas gifts for you and Gary also your mother has made up a parcel of food for you to last over the holiday, so when will you be in?" he enquired.

Her answer was brief and the arrangements were made so I rang the girls to inform them of our intent and to give them the chance to give any gift should they want to. It was no surprise to me that both Emma and Holly had also wanted to get gifts for her, and so did Mum.

James on the other hand, never very good with paying out for presents, had not even thought about it, and as he was still very angry with her I decided that it was best left alone. He had been very affected by Louise's actions at the funeral and was finding it very hard to come to terms with the events of the past few years. He was very sceptical that she would ever be able to beat her addiction, as the only other experience we had about this subject had been the twenty year struggle my friend had with her son, and as far as he was concerned all drug addicted adults never became clean. I also did not want him to go back to that depressed young man as he was back to being the cheeky chappie he always was, so my decision to not involve him was for the best I felt.

With the car boot full of goodies Ryan set off with all the families contributions, and I sat alone in the kitchen feeling happy at the thought of Louise having enough to eat at Christmas, but feeling bad at not going to see her, and disappointed at my lack of courage.

Time seemed to go very slowly that afternoon and I even managed to clean the kitchen cupboards out, just to kill time, until Ryan got back.

My kitchen was well overdue a good tidy up and by the time I had finished the whole room sparkled.

At last Ryan appeared grinning all over his face.

"Well how was it?" I asked trying not to sound too enthusiastic.

"She was well and looking good" he answered putting on the kettle, as a cup of coffee was foremost on his mind, and he had never been one to give off information without prompting, "and?" I was getting impatient

"She is waiting to go into re-hab, and Gary is starting his detox next year probably February time. They are both still on methadone but are getting help from their mental health and key workers." Seeing the relief on my face Ryan smiled and continued "We will see and I hope it comes to pass."

Christmas was upon us and in the morning Louise called us and wished us a happy Christmas and thanked us for the gifts. I spoke to her for a few moments, because now she was trying to get better, I felt justified in breaking the silence that we had between us for so long. She told me Gary had his date to go in, but she had to wait as her methadone dose was still too high for them to detox her safely.

"I am trying hard Mum to get the medication decreased as soon as I can because I really want to stop this life I hate so much." She said.

"Also I have looked into going to university when I am clean on a part time basis, and hope to get a fine art degree, as I would like to be an art therapist.

This was a complete surprise to me, my daughter was talking coherently, and seemed to be planning a future for herself.

It was the best Christmas gift I could have been given, and hoped that it would come to fruition. From that moment on I was determined whatever happened I would never walk away from her again. February was going to be the month that Gary's life would hopefully change and I felt happy that I had spoken to her about it. New Year's Eve came and went.

Over the past few years we had no real reason to celebrate a new year as we had come to the conclusion long ago that if things are going well there will always be a disaster waiting to emerge around the corner, and when you get through a good patch you cannot sit back, as again the circle continues and another problem normally arises. I had become very pessimistic and was not proud of myself for feeling that way. All through this ordeal I had the support of family friends as well as neighbours, everyone around us seemed to want to help and I was touched by the warmth conveyed by close friends and acquaintances alike.

I even had a neighbour who had her own problems, take time to comfort me when things were bad. We was truly blessed and felt very lucky and hoped that one day we would be able to say to all our friends and family that our daughter was clean at last.

# Chapter 17

## THE REHAB BEGINS

*F*ebruary arrived and we were informed by Lou that Gary had been admitted into the local clinic to start his detox. We were concerned that the stress of Gary being separated from her would make her vulnerable, as she had not been alone for a long time. We need not have worried as she was allowed to visit every day and stay as long as she liked. She watched first-hand what coming off methadone would mean in terms of the withdrawal symptoms.

She had already been through this before, and she had an idea what to expect, like the cold sweats, diarrhoea, sickness, and general severe flu symptoms that Gary was enduring.

Nothing however could have prepared her for the violent reaction that he suffered as a result of coming off methadone, and there were many times he wanted to give up but I was so proud of him as he fought to keep the treatment going. This frightened her and she was not looking forward to starting her own detox, but as the days progressed Gary emerged unscathed and after two weeks was clean and off methadone.

For the first time since we had met him we would finally get to know the young man he really was, not the unfeeling drug addict he had been. Louise on the other hand was still waiting for her slot. Gary was getting on fine but needed counselling, as he was now beginning to experience the feelings he had been able to suppress for so long, but it was very sparse, and he only had the support of key workers once a month, when they could fit him in.

There were so many clients that it was a lottery to get the proper help.

The waiting list was long as they had to cater for all addiction, not just drugs.

Alcohol, Gambling, and Mental Health seemed to have priority, and it was beyond me how anyone could expect someone who had just come off drugs, to get a job, and function normally as if it had never happened.

The odd counselling sessions were inadequate as intense therapy to ensure Gary did not go back on drugs was more liable to succeed.

In our view you cannot just treat the symptoms but need to get to the root cause.

Once again I felt they missed the point, although I knew it was simply the lack of resources, and trained counsellors, dictating when each case was taken on.

The key workers also made it very clear that couples do not usually stay clean as it is more difficult for the one that's recovering when the other is using.

The word recovering means exactly that, it takes years to recover, so help must be on going or Gary would be in danger of re-using.

We helped him as best we could, ferrying him backwards and forwards to his appointments with various agencies.

One of the side effects of taking methadone is that it gets into the bones and because they have to add so much sugar it sometimes rots the teeth.

Unfortunately for Gary his teeth were badly damaged and he now was beginning to experience pain. This was a shock to him as for years this sensation was numbed.

He also began to relive his childhood and all the past traumas he had experienced began to haunt him, and this time there was no pain killer to ease his suffering. Other symptoms began to emerge, we noticed he was unable to cope in any environment that he was not familiar with. Even coming to visit us was a trauma and we were concerned that he was becoming agoraphobic.

Lou was very patient with him and we were pleasantly surprised that Gary was becoming quite close to us, and I began to really become fond of him.

Louise called me in the March to inform me that she was going in to the clinic.

I was over the moon and we talked for an age on the phone at what it would be like to not have to go to the chemist every day to take her methadone, to not worry anymore about finding drugs, to start a new life, to go to college and get a fine art degree, yes she was thinking about her future and for once I really truly believed her.

"Don't visit me Mum as I will be in a state and I do not want you to see me like that" she pleaded with me.

"I won't I said but I will be thinking of you"

"Can you do something for me Mum?" Louise asked

"What do you want?" I replied wary of the answer.

"Can you check on Gary as he is doing well but he needs to know he is not alone?"

"Of course I can Louise, just make sure you concentrate on getting clean and everything will be ok," I answered.

Then she said something that filled me with emotion

"I love you Mum" she whispered as the phone went down.

How long had it been since those words had been said between us?

I was so excited that I rang everyone I could think of to tell them that my beautiful daughter was on her way back from a dark place and she was going to be ok at last! Ryan had now got used to coming home and actually going to bed and having a good night's sleep, this evening was different and we sat up most of the night happily talking about Lou's future as now we felt she had one.

I called round to see Gary most days and drove him to the clinic to see her, and he kept us informed gave on Louise's progress.

Louise like Gary was very sick coming off methadone, and she did not escape the same violent withdrawal symptoms, but she stuck to it knowing she could have walked out at any time. We were getting closer to Gary now and he was talking more, he had also started to see his father and they were on better terms as Gary was not living under the same roof, therefore not in the firing line anymore. I do not doubt that his father loved him but again he was an addict and he changed when drink took over him.

At last Louise was discharged, methadone free, weak and emotional but free from drugs for the first time in seven years. Now approaching twenty one she was ready to change her life. With the exception of James all the family started to rally round and applaud her and Gary for the way they were trying to face their demons.

James still needed time, and he was very sceptical as he had seen it all before, and he was afraid that if he allowed himself to get too close to her she would let him down and he could not bear to lose her again.

It's funny but I asked Louise if she craved heroin, and she said no, it was methadone she craved, and to feel pain and emotion was a very new thing for them both.

Gary was beginning to have problems about his childhood and rejection, and Louise now had to face the memory of the rape. She was also feeling very guilty at the way she had abused herself and her family, these feelings no longer numbed by drugs. I remember the first time I saw her after her stint in re-hab, she was so thin and pale, very emotional, I just held her close, I was not looking at a twenty year old drug addict I was hugging my dear daughter who had just come back to me, and I felt good.

We managed to find a counsellor who was expert in treating drug abuse victims and she accepted Louise for weekly sessions to help her come to terms with everything, she also taught her life skills and how to act when certain situations arose that Louise found difficult to cope with. Gary was not so fortunate but again he managed to get his mental health worker to give him extra therapy.

Ryan and I were so proud of them both, but we knew that support for them would be on going for a long time.

Louise had started studying for her art degree at college on a part time basis.

She still had many appointments to attend and was not yet fully recovered from her ordeal, so it was the best way for her to gradually get back to normal life.

Part of the recovery plan is regular blood and urine tests so that they are monitored and any problems that may arise can be dealt with immediately

Through long term needle use both Louise and Gary had collapsed veins and Louise had also suffered thrombosis through infections from needles.

Every time she went to her doctor they tried to get blood from her to make sure she was clean and it became impossible to use the arms, so feet, neck, and groin were used.

I can remember going with her to see the blood nurse, she had seen this particular nurse before and she had been less than sympathetic when trying to take Louise's blood. It was a painful experience for her as her veins were not large enough to give much blood at all, this did not seem to worry the nurse and after the sixth attempt another nurse had to try, needless to say Louise dreaded the appointment.

I decided to go along with her to give a bit of moral support. The clinic was at its normal maximum capacity and we settled down for a long wait.

Names were called and the monitor on the wall said 1 hour wait. As we sat there people were jostled in and out of the cubicles, most with a solemn look on their faces, but with the deed done, they trotted out all smiles and showing off the round plaster that covered the pin prick.

Then Louise's name was called and we walked into the cubicle. Without looking up the nurse beckoned Louise to sit on the chair as she looked at her notes. "Oh your one of those" she said still not looking at my daughter.

Louise said nothing but I did not intend to let her talk in such a way to my daughter.

"One of what?" I answered in a very precise manner. With that she looked up startled and said. "Oh I mean that she is difficult to get blood from" she answered in a quiet voice

"I had a lot of trouble last time as her veins have collapsed through her needle use. "Yes I know, Louise was very upset the last time she came as she felt that you had a problem with her"

By now I was in full flow and was determined to make sure this nurse would understand that she had no right to be judgmental, and was there purely to take blood. After denying having any problem with her at all, she turned towards the door saying, "I will get a specialist nurse down to do it," and left us waiting for another 30minutes.

I had become very sensitive over every remark made to Louise, and this probably clouded my judgement so I may have been a bit harsh in my attitude to the nurse. Louise was happy though as the specialist was very kind and took a couple of minutes almost pain free to extract her precious liquid.

"Thanks Mum" said Louise and gave me a hug.

It was sad that even when you get clean and are trying to stay that way by attending all appointments, the stigma of drug addiction takes a long time if ever to cease from not only the general public but from a minority of the professionals.

Both Gary and Louise were still very tired all the time and unable to sleep at night. Mood swings as well as violent cravings were on a daily basis, but they coped the best way they could. I remember saying to her, pain is normal and you will have to live with that. We had promised her a car if she managed to pass her test so that she could travel to her college. We had done the same for all our children and we were so pleased to be able at last to do this for her.

She lived in a rural area without good public transport, so it seemed a sensible idea, and it saved us from driving both her and Gary to their appointments.

Needless to say we paid for her lessons and she passed first time.

James was now beginning to trust his sister and we gently started to get them together to spend time with each other. Having James check her car over, and give her advice about maintaining it helped a lot, so we were confident he was feeling better about it all, and Gary had also started to bond with him.

Then one day Gary went to see his doctor about feeling tired and unwell, it had always been put down to the drug abuse and his old lifestyle, but this time it was more than just fatigue, he had also been having a lot of infections.

Then whilst on a visit to us suddenly there was a loud crack and Gary had collapsed onto the floor and seemed to be having a fit. The seizure seemed to go on for more than a couple of minutes. We called an ambulance and he was rushed into hospital with Louise following in our car, hysterical and both Ryan and I in a state of shock.

After many tests and a few days in hospital Gary was allowed home and we waited for the results. Then there was some news that would once again rock our world.

"Hello Mum" Louise was trembling in her voice

"What is it" I asked, really scared this time.

"Gary has Hepatitis C," she said, "and they want to test me for it too"

"Ok then I will come with you to the doctors when you have your results is that ok Louise?" I was trying to stay calm and not sound too troubled by the news.

"That will be great Mum I will be in touch with you when they are in."

And with that she hung up. For what seemed an age I sat in the lounge just not being able to take it in, then I went on the websites to find out as much as I could about it and what the cure was.

By the time Ryan came home I was distraught, it was the worst news, my beautiful daughter now may have a life threatening disease and I could not bear to lose her now after all she had been through.

So for the next few days I waited and prayed that she had been saved from this new threat. No such luck it was confirmed that she had it too, so now we had to see a liver specialist to find out the next step in her recovery.

## Chapter 18

### NO QUICK FIX

*L*ou had her first encounter with the liver specialist within two weeks, and I went along with her. Gary had to wait longer for an appointment for he had to go into an assessment centre as they were concerned for his mental health. We arrived at the desk and were immediately sent into the waiting room.

Our appointment was for 10am and we were still waiting at 11am, watching other people file in and out of the consulting room. After much huffing and puffing, and looking at our watches, the door suddenly opened and a slightly built man emerged carrying a large carrier bag of which I could see contained many boxes of prescription drugs. At least we knew we were next, and after what seemed an age we were called into the room.

As we sat together in the consulting room the doctor explained to us in full what Louise was suffering from. Apparently there are a few geno types to Hepatitis C and they had to discover the geno type she had. They also wanted to find out how her was liver functioning, and see what damage had already been done and what shape she was in. This would involve many blood tests, and knowing how much she hated that procedure, Lou was now looking very concerned. We had hoped that the treatment would start there and then, but we had not realised the dreaded blood samples had to be taken first.

Then Louise was told that she would have to have a liver biopsy. The specialist proceeded to tell us what that entailed. "I will make you an appointment to attend the day surgery unit, and you will need someone with you," he explained. "Will I be put to sleep?" Asked Lou hopefully. "No we will give you a local anaesthetic around the area and then a long needle will be inserted to extract a minute piece of your liver, it only takes a couple of minutes." He answered, noticing Louise's concerned expression. "There is however a good reason why we will want you to rest after the procedure, as your liver could bleed and we would not want that to happen, so that is why we insist that someone is with you" he explained. His last words worried me but it had to be done before any treatment would start. Louise then asked the question that I had wanted to ask, but felt I could not while she was there. "Will you be able cure it?" she asked. Turning and looking her in the eyes he said very calmly. "I cannot give you the answer until I have all the results but there are some geno types that can be cured easier than others, the treatment will probably take six months, but we will talk about that when we have all the results of your tests in four weeks." Then turning to the computer he typed out the list of blood tests to be done and handed the paper to Louise to take to the nurses. Here we go again I thought, and I braced myself for the traumatic experience that would follow.

A week went by and we received the appointment for her to attend the surgery for her biopsy. I went with her as she was very nervous, and on entering the hospital she began to have a panic attack, and I was unsure whether she would be able to go through with it. After a while I managed to calm her down and we met the surgeon. He was very quiet in his manner, and talked Lou through the procedure, answering all her questions and promising her that he would not hurt her.

I sat on the other side of the bed holding her hand as the anaesthetic was introduced around the area Louise was trembling and trying so hard not to cry, and I was finding it equally difficult to stay composed. Lou had her back to him so was unable to see the length of the needle, I was not so lucky, and trying not to give anything away I found myself patting her outstretched hand and whispering just relax.

I need not have worried, for as soon as the needle had been inserted into her side, there was a loud clicking sound, then the needle was withdrawn, and it was all over before Lou had a chance to flinch. Now the deed done Louise and I settled down for a long wait before she would be discharged. We stayed in the unit most of the day, to make sure she had not had any internal bleeding, and when the doctor was satisfied she was going to be ok, she would be sent home. The time was going very slowly and after exhausting all the magazines Lou suddenly started to talk to me about what she had witnessed when she was at her lowest.

I was totally transfixed as she gave me her account of events leading up to her arrest for suspected trafficking of drugs. Apparently she had gone to a dealers flat to score, as she put it, and there were a few people injecting while she was there. One girl that had since died, stabbed herself in the face with her needle as she was so out of it. Lou explained that she had seen such terrible scenes including addicts overdosing, and even said she thought she had once seen a boy die from his drug abuse, but was not sure as she was high on drugs herself and this had become her way of life. Then without warning, the police had raided the flat arresting all including Louise. She was bundled into a police car and taken down to the station but luckily for her she was not prosecuted as they knew who the real hardened dealers were and that was all they were interested in.

We then talked about Gary and how he had always been there for her. "He really is a good person Mum," she said and giving me a warm smile, "He just got lost for a while like me." She added. That was a good description of it I thought, they were both lost souls that had come together at the right time and helped each other through some life changing events, and were still determined to win through together.

We had a spot of lunch before the ward round, and as luck would have it Lou was discharged with a clean bill of health feeling bruised but proud of herself for going through with it. Louise was also doing well at college and every moment she had spare she would be painting or writing in her sketch book. Although it was becoming a bit of an obsession with her, I felt it was a good sign as it was keeping her mind off her health problems, so not all addictions were bad I thought. Four weeks passed very slowly,

Gary was now out of the unit and feeling better and he was awaiting his appointment with the liver specialist. He had also started to think about his future and decided to help Ryan in the garden by painting the decking and wooden shed. He seemed to love helping out and we enjoyed his company.

The day finally arrived and Louise and I checked in at the reception. Once again we waited an hour, but this time we were in no hurry to get the results, as we were both dreading the news. On entering the room we sat quietly in front of the doctor and waited for the results. "Well Louise I have some good news for you, your geno type is three and this is one of the easier types to cure." He was smiling at Lou as he gave the news. We looked at each other and I felt positive for once, could we be leaving the room with a carrier bag of medication? I thought. Then the doctor hit us with something we didn't expect, he explained that Louise's immune system was showing signs of being on the low side, and her platelets were not good so further tests had to be done. He then began to explain why her low immune system could be a problem, as the treatment they could offer was called interferon.

It had many side effects that were similar to chemotherapy. This included thinning or loss of hair, fatigue, and depression. The most crucial side effect was that it would also cause a low immune system, so if she were to start the treatment already being low, she could be prone to infections. The after effects, he explained, could also leave her with diabetes, and other complications.

So this treatment was very radical and would not be taken on unless the patient was fit enough to cope, not only physically but mentally as well. The treatment would take six months and the interferon would be taken in tablet form three times a day and injected once a week into Lou's abdomen. "I can't do that, cried Lou, I can't inject myself not after my past," she was clearly panicking, and I had to think of something to make sure she would accept the treatment. "I will do it," I said, hardly believing those words had come out of my mouth I continued, "can I do that for her?"

I was secretly hoping that they would do it at the surgery. After a short pause he smiled and said yes we will show you how to do it."

"When do we start?" I asked, trying not to sound alarmed. "Well not until we are sure that Louise will be able to tolerate the interferon and also her mental state is important as we will not even attempt to start until she is in tip top form as this treatment is severe." "But at least she would be cured." I remarked hopefully. "Well we hope so, he replied "but we can go around again if it doesn't work. The first time."

This was like a bullet out of nowhere, I had assumed that she would be cured and to be told she may not was a shock, but I managed to just act as though it was no problem and sat quietly watching Louise shake as she was told another lot of blood was to be taken. This went on for over four months blood being taken every week, liver being monitored, diet being changed, and endless consultations with the psychotherapist to make sure she would be able to cope mentally with the treatment. In between all this she managed to keep up with her studies, and at the same time support Gary with his now impending tests to see if he was well enough to start treatment as well. She had also continued to commute to and from college not wanting to fall behind and this helped her to keep positive, as it left her no time to dwell on the impending treatment.

One good bit of news was that she was now being sent to see a specialist nurse to take her blood so it was becoming easier for her, although her foot was used more than her arm. Gary on the other hand was having his taken from his neck and groin. It was worrying to be told that normally if a young person contracts hepatitis it usually stays dormant for years, but for some reason her one had become active very early. All we kept hearing was you have been unlucky Louise. There was an outing being arranged at her college for students to go on a tour of art galleries in London and Louise was looking forward to it. Previously to that, she had confided in one of her tutors to warn them that if she was unwell at any time whilst at college she hoped she would understand and allow her to go home if need be. She explained about her condition and was very precise in her explanation of her understanding of blood contamination.

She wanted to assure the tutor that she was no threat to her peers, and that she took every precaution to follow the right procedures for infection control should the unlikely event of her cutting herself happen. This was the only way the she could infect another person, and even then, the other person would have to be bleeding too. Louise had also given her a leaflet explaining all about the condition. She said that she would look at it and thanked her for the information. Thinking that was the end of it Lou turned up at the college the following week only to be summoned for a meeting with the tutor.

"I have decided that you will be a risk to others and suggest that you do not go on this trip" she said, looking at Louise with a sullen stare. She continued. "Also I think that until you are cured it may be better if you take time out from college as we cannot take the risk that you could be a danger to everyone else that comes in contact with you." Louise sat in stunned silence, the tutor had obviously not looked at the information given and was reacting in a hysterical way, it left my daughter absolutely distraught and feeling very betrayed as she had not had to inform the college in the first place. Needless to say I had a phone call that evening from a sobbing girl trying to make sense of her tutor's reaction. I was furious and told her that I would write a letter of complaint and that she would not have to give up her course.

As soon as the receiver was placed down I was on a mission. I was determined to explain to this woman that rather than give a knee jerk reaction to something she clearly had not grasped, she should understand that infection control applied to everyone whether they had HIV or a common cold. They only had to look at the professional healthcare workers that had HIV or Hepatitis virus, and they were no risk to the public, also were not obliged to inform anyone of their illness. You always assume that everyone can infect you, so precautions would always be taken and correct procedures followed. The letter was one of my best and I sat back pleased that for once I had been able to tell someone in authority, the importance of research before condemning. With the letter duly sent I waited for a reply. I did not have to wait long as I received and answer within a week. We had a full apology and were informed that the tutor had been sent on a course to understand infection control and learn about hepatitis. At last we had won a small battle but for Lou it was a realisation that she was not always the one in the wrong and she felt good.

Ryan was busy at work and had not been able to see Lou as much as he wanted to but I kept him up to speed on the everyday events. One evening he came in and gave me the local paper, he had been reading it on the train and was very sorry to see the headlines as it showed the death of a local young man who had been found dead in the local public toilets from a suspected drug overdose. "I read this and thought how lucky we are that this is not our daughter," he said as he passed it to me to read. As I scanned the page I suddenly felt cold, there was a small photograph of his parents and I immediately recognised them as the couple I had met in the drug advisory centre so many years ago.

It was so sad to see that their journey had ended this way. The thought of them going to the centre at every opportunity just so they could see their son and try and get him help was soul destroying for me, as this could so easily have been the outcome for us. The photo showed the same look of despair that I had seen on their faces when we met, and I wept for them.

# Chapter 19

## BACK TO REALITY

*W*hile waiting to hear her latest results Ryan gave me some money to take her out to get some shoes as he noticed she was walking around in broken down heels. I did not have to be told twice and we set off to the shops to have a nice girls day out. As I walked into a department store Louise held back, I turned around and she was still outside. Try as I might she refused to enter and in the end had to tell me she was not allowed to go in as she had been arrested for shop lifting and had been given a life's ban and would be arrested again if she attempted to cross the threshold. I was stunned but did not want to make an issue of it, we had come too far for that, so I simply said that we could shop elsewhere. Lou seemed relieved that I was not going to throw a fit over her admission and proceeded to give me a list of other shops she had to steer clear of.

With the shoes and other items of clothing bought we made our way home having had a wonderful time, it had been years since we had spent time together as mother and daughter. When she saw her father she proudly showed off her new clothes and thanked him for all he did for her, and this filled me with pride as Louise was again back to the loving girl she always was. The day did not end without drama though I am sorry to say.

As she drove out of the drive Ryan and I watched her go and were pleased that we seemed to be connecting with each other again, then our drive suddenly had another car appear parked, it was Emma, popping round for a coffee I thought, but as she entered the kitchen there was no usual Yoo-hoo from her lips. After greeting his daughter, Ryan made a quick exit as he was now recognising the signs and was expecting that we would be up all night again discussing another revelation about Louise.

We always assumed it would be about her, but not this time. Emma came in and started crying, her son Alex had been shop lifting and also been stealing from her. It had been going on for a long time but because of our problems she had been keeping it to herself and trying to deal with it alone. Her new partner had tried to help her but Alex had also stolen from him and it was getting difficult for her relationship.

He had always been hard work as his hyperactivity had been at best overwhelming sometimes, and at the expense of his younger brother had taken a lot of her attention to keep him on the straight and narrow. Emma by now had to ask herself why this was happening as he had lost a lot of weight, his personal appearance had deteriorated, and he could not keep a job.

His attitude was unacceptable as he did not recognise that he was at fault and always denied having stolen anything even when he had been caught out. I was hearing a familiar story and both Emma and I knew that it had to be more than a coincidence that his behaviour was becoming the same as what his aunts had been.

I recognised myself in her next statement, like me she was looking for any other reason that he could be acting this, as she was saying that she thought he might just be depressed, or it was to do with his ADHD.

Alex had been taking Ritalin for most of his life as he was unable to concentrate on anything for too long without it. He was a bright young man and very intelligent so had been very frustrated with his condition, as it had also affected his bladder, so he had wet the bed every night since birth. I felt so sorry for him as he had to be very careful when staying overnight with his friends and would wear a disposable nappy under his pyjamas. When he became sixteen he stopped taking his medication as he did not think he needed it anymore, and at that age, we knew from experience that he could do what he liked, and Emma would not be able to make him take his medication.

I had once asked him what he felt like when he did not take his Ritalin, and he tried to explain that when he was in the classroom trying to listen to the teacher, he would also pick up on all the other noises around him like, cars going past the window, shuffling feet, the noise in the corridor, and any other quiet conversation from his other classmates, all these different sounds became a mish mash in his head so he was unable to concentrate on what the teacher was saying.

Emma continued to tell me what she had been going through and I could not believe what I was hearing, surely lightening could not have struck twice? and felt very guilty that my eldest daughter had been silently going through the same sort of situation alone, not considering herself just getting on with it. All I wanted to do was cuddle my strong, dear daughter and hoped I would be able to support her as much as she had me through her troubled time. Emma then told me her son had informed her that afternoon that he was going to move out and live in a bedsit with his mates as he did not want to live at home being accused of all these crimes. She did not know what to do as he was only seventeen, and she was more afraid that if he did leave he would get into more mischief and end up in prison.

I was the last person to give good advice I thought, but we talked it over and she decided to let him go as he was out of control at home and either way he would get into trouble whether he was with her or not.

I had learnt a long time ago an important lesson, you can unwittingly enable an addict to use, by giving them the comforts of home while they indulge in their habit. The only way it had worked for us is that we had to let Lou do her own thing as she would have done that anyway for we had no control over her actions, and nor did my dear Emma. None of us knew how it would turn out and I felt for my daughter.

Once again all the family were informed and rallied round. Timmy had become very anti his brother and angry that he had started to possibly take drugs knowing what we had already been through with Louise. Emma was now going to concentrate on him a bit more for like us she had not been able to give him the attention she would have liked as his brother had taken all her energy. I just prayed that we were wrong and he was just going through adolescence. In the meantime all I could do was to be a listening ear for my daughter, knowing exactly how she was feeling.

When she left I ventured upstairs to speak to my ever enduring husband, he had made up a flask of coffee, knowing another long talk was inevitable, and through it all we looked at each other and joked about the fact that there was never a dull moment in our household, we just wished it was more positive.

After seeing the specialist on her next visit, it was decided Lou was as ready as she would ever be to go for her treatment, as her tests although not perfect seemed good enough to chance starting her on interferon and all we had to do was wait for her appointment.

At last the letter arrived, Louise was to start her treatment and we were to see the specialist in a week's time, to say we were relieved was an understatement, both Louise and I looked forward to getting started and ultimately hoped her recovery would not be too long in coming. Both Ryan and I made plans to have her stay over on the nights that she had to have her injections so that any ill effects would be dealt with and Louise would feel safe. Holly and Emma sent her texts wishing her good luck, and James got a get well card for her. This was a first and Louise decided to frame it, I was pleased he was beginning to warm to her.

Getting back to my declaration of giving the injections, I had for a while been putting that to the back of my mind, but now it was becoming a reality, and I could not let her down. How I was going to manage to do it was a really scary thought, but I was going to be trained so felt that I would overcome my fears. Ryan said he was so proud of me to volunteer to do it, as he would not have been able to do it, I dared not tell him I did not think I would be able to do it either, so I just smiled and said it was ok.

The day arrived and we waited patiently for the door to open into the consulting room. Louise was quiet and I sucked mints and tried to read a magazine that was four years old. Suddenly her name was called and we entered the room. After going through the drugs that she would have to take on a daily basis, we then came to the question of the injections. "I understand you will be giving the injections." The specialist was looking at me over the top of his glasses "Yes I replied, trying to sound confident "Good, you must always give them at the same time every week and straight into the abdomen, making sure you alternate the area every time, also give the injection at an angle not straight in, and remember to warm the phial in your hand to make it more comfortable for Louise." And without pausing he handed me the syringe and showed me how to fix the needle, flick the syringe to get rid of any air bubbles and slowly release the liquid. He continued, "The area must always be clean and when you withdraw the needle put a small plaster on to avoid any blood oozing, after a few days a red ring will appear around the area and that is to be avoided when you next inject"

By now I was really panicking inside, it seemed so much to remember. "That should be all you need to know but do you have any questions?" Without hesitation I answered "No questions" and smiled.

Why had I said that? I had loads of questions but for some reason just let them go. Lou looked at me and I knew she trusted me, so I had to be confident that I would be able to do the deed.

We arranged the day that we would always give the injections and Louise started taking her daily tablet intake, there were so many, interferon injections, and the same in tablet form which was called ribavirin, anti-depressants, anti-sickness, and sleeping tablets.

Interferon mixed with the ribavirin the doctor explained helped the immune system to stop the virus from multiplying and aided the body to rid itself of infected cells. I had also asked if she could take milk thistle, a natural herb that was for liver function. I had looked on the internet and milk thistle was shown to be beneficial for liver health and was recommended for

Hepatitis C sufferers. I had begun to spend a lot of time researching on the internet and got a lot of insight into all the different alternative therapies for Hepatitis. The specialist was happy for her to take these along with her medication so I was confident that they were helping, and at the same time Gary was also able to try them.

Friday arrived and I got the spare room ready and Lou arrived with her injections. As it is such a controlled drug it was delivered by courier and had to be signed for. We had been given four weeks' worth so they were put in the fridge and we waited until the evening for me to give her the first injection. I felt sick inside, I was worried more than anything that I would hurt her, or make a complete mess of it and she would have to do it. Louise had her bath, and while she was getting ready for bed I got out the swabs, plaster, syringe, and needle case, laying them all out on the bedside table and washed my hands. "Are you ready now Mum?" Lou asked "Yes" I replied, not meaning that at all. I held the phial to warm it up, so far so good, then took the needle out of the case and mounted it onto the syringe. I flicked the syringe, and removed the stopper from the point of the needle. In the meantime Louise sat herself on the bed and lifted her top. I pushed the liquid up to the required dose and then after wiping the area with a sterile swab, pinched her flesh on the part that was to be injected, it was now or never, I was going to have to do it.

In my mind I was thinking, clean the area, put the needle in not straight but at an angle, press plunger slowly, withdraw gently and put on the plaster. "I am ready Mum" and she closed her eyes. I took a deep breath, slowly put the needle in at an angle, pressed the plunger and in an instance it was done, I had done it! As I put on the plaster Louise opened her eyes and said, "Mum that was painless thank you." I was near to collapse but overjoyed at achieving what I considered impossible for me. From now on together we could achieve anything I thought. Louise seemed ok after her ordeal and over the weeks we had a ritual of bath, injection and chocolate after, for both of us.

Then one day she felt unwell, she was running a high temperature and the doctor sent her straight to hospital, she was suffering from a severe infection and was very ill for seven days, the treatment had to be halted for a month but Louise fought well and came through it. After commencing it again four weeks passed and she showed signs of fatigue, hair loss, and high temperature, her blood samples were showing dangerously low platelets and her immune system was very weak, but she was determined to continue, then one morning she awoke unable to breath. Gary was so worried he called the doctor and she was blue lighted into hospital and put in intensive care.

By the time we reached the hospital the specialist was with her, and he told us that she had pneumonia and that her interferon treatment would have to be stopped immediately as she could die. We were distraught, I did not even consider the fact that the treatment itself could be the cause of her death, we just seemed to continually take one step forward and two steps back. We sat by her bedside watching her fall in and out of consciousness, tubes everywhere, even a line in her neck for they had to get strong antibiotics into her quickly, and knowing some veins in her arms had collapsed and weak the only solution for them was going straight into her neck.

Gary was beside himself with worry, so we took him home with us just so that he would not have to be alone in the flat. I was very privileged and grateful to have good friends and neighbours around us. Especially my next door neighbours Helen and Robert. He was a retired doctor and Helen a midwife, they had moved in a few years before and we had hit it off immediately. They had a son called Brandon who was just a year older than Louise, and he had become good friends with James. When they were together they always had good fun as they both had the same interests and loved playing at being soldiers. I remembered the time when Brandon and James both decided to dress up and play soldiers in the field behind our houses. Both had camouflage trousers on and toy rifles. James ever being creative, had adapted a couple of knitted hats into balaclavas, by cutting holes in them for their eyes and mouth. With a packed lunch in their rucksacks they set of to kill the enemy. Unfortunately the war ended sooner than they expected as another neighbour spotted them and thought they were suspicious characters trying to break into someone's house. She did not call the police though as she suddenly recognised the sound of Brandon's deep voice calling James to get his sandwiches out of the bag. She rang Helen and was assured that they were innocent. I smiled to myself recalling a fed up young boy returning home with a few ladders where the balaclava had run, travelling towards his eyes.

Since the beginning of our problems both Helen and Robert had been a good sounding board for any medical advice not only about Louise but my father as well, and now Lou was in trouble again, helped us through this latest threat. Louise remained in hospital for two weeks and when she was discharged we went to see the specialist, and he dropped the biggest bombshell to us, he said that she could not continue with any more treatment as it might kill her, and therefore she would have to wait for other drugs to be trailed. Louise pleaded for him to let her finish saying she would stay with us, but her immune system was shot to pieces and she would not have been able to tolerate anymore. They took the usual blood tests to find out how the virus was reacting, and once again we went home disappointed. Our beautiful daughter just did not seem to have any luck and keeping her positive was proving very hard. It took a long time for her to get over the pneumonia and for a while she was very low in spirit. The next appointment with the specialist was due and I went with her.

On entering the room both Lou and I saw that the doctor was sitting back in his chair looking very pleased and smiling at us. I could not understand what he had to smile about as my daughters treatment had been stopped therefore dooming her to have to wait and hope for a new treatment to become available. We made our way to the seats provided and waited for the results of her tests. The specialist turned to Lou and said, "The results of your blood test shows that the virus has disappeared from your liver, it seems to have eradicated it completely." Both Lou and I did not know what to say as we were both in shock. "We will have to take another test in three months to see if it comes back but we are hopeful that it will not." He added. After his last statement I asked if it usually came back and he explained that he had only ever seen patients cured after the full six months and Louise had only managed three months' worth of treatment so did not want to put our hopes up too much, but he added that the signs were very favourable. We left the surgery in a daze, could it really be true? had she beaten this disease? time would tell and we were both nervous over the results of the next blood test. One thing was for sure, Ryan would be coming home to good news for a change.

# *Chapter 20*

## OUTCOMES

*I* was brought back to reality with the sound of applause. The table where I was seated was near the front of the auditorium. The college band had been playing various styles of music, and were now getting seated ready for the speeches. There was still one seat beside me that was vacant, and I put my handbag on it in case someone sat there.

After the formalities the graduation parade began. All the students that where graduating had been summoned to the back of the hall, and instructed to stand in an orderly fashion waiting to be called to receive their respective diplomas. All manner of different awards were being given and as I sat there I noticed a bright faced girl at the back, she was looking straight at me. Her pretty eyes sparkling, her cupid bow lips smiling, and my heart was filled with pride as I looked at my beautiful daughter as she slowly made her way to the front of the queue.

The announcements were being made describing what each individual had achieved from and their chosen subject. "Hey there's Lou!" The Goth that had been sitting the other side of me suddenly jumped up and waved his arms. Louise smiled back and put her hand in the air as if to say I'm here. "She's in my friends tutor group, and is really talented," he added shoving another cupcake in his mouth whilst talking to the lady that he had arrived with. He had already been up to receive his award for Aerospace Engineering. I soon realised that the woman he was with was indeed his mother as she scolded him over how much cake he had put in his mouth, and turned to me raising her eyebrows.

I smiled and said nothing waiting and hoping that Ryan would make it in the nick of time, and he didn't disappoint. Just as the queue was coming to an end, I felt his arm around me and after removing my bag, plonked himself in the spare seat beside me. "Has she been called yet?" he asked, as he reached for an egg and cress sandwich. "You're just in time" I replied, passing him the ever emptying plate of cupcakes.

Then all at once from the man holding the microphone there was an announcement. The award for Foundation Degree in Contemporary Fine Art goes to Miss Louise Welsh. We turned and watched our daughter walk the length of the hall, smiling as she walked by us. She received her diploma shook the principals hand and the official photos were taken. Then, just as she had descended back down the stairs, there was another announcement from the man on the stage. "Ladies and gentlemen, Louise achieved her foundation art degree with distinctions, whilst overcoming personal and serious health problems. This is truly a great achievement so the panel voted to give this apt recognition. Therefore it gives me great pleasure to award Louise with the prize for student of the year."

With that said he lifted up a silver cup and waited to give it to her. She had been informed that she would be honoured with this prize but had kept it a secret from us.

Before I knew it I was on my feet applauding my daughter, Ryan was cheering, and the rest of the family including Gary, that had been standing at the back of the hall, were clapping and calling her name. As she climbed the steps to the stage to accept her prize she looked over to me and smiled the most beautiful smile, I knew instantly she was back for good. This had been a day to remember for so many reasons. The specialist had rung her in the morning before the ceremony to give her the latest results of her blood tests and let her know that the interferon seemed to have wiped out the hepatitis from her body after only half the treatment. Her blood test result had come back and the virus had not returned he said it had never happened before to his knowledge. We know she will have to be monitored for more than a year as they cannot guarantee that it will not recur but we are staying positive and believe she has beaten it.

This had been the most difficult time in our lives and we were finally coming to the end result that we prayed for but never dared to hope for. For nearly ten years we had been fighting one way or another to try and rescue our beloved daughter from a living hell. Ultimately Louise had been the one to overcome, and had never given up trying to change her life for the better. We had only supported her as best we could while making many mistakes, and on occasion I had been very unfair to the professionals that had been trying to help her, and for this I felt sorry. What had we learned as a family? I pondered about this as I looked towards the back of the hall, there they all were, happy and delighted for their sister. What she had achieved had been beyond all their expectations. For the first time in a long time we were all together, celebrating as a complete family. We had learnt that staying united we would be able to overcome anything. Louise will always have that addiction gene or whatever label they put on it, but she recognises it and deals with it day to day.

I am confident that if she ever has a problem she will now not be afraid to come to us, as she knows that we will always do what we can to help her. As the applause faded and another students name was called out, Louise came bounding over to us and at the same time the family at the back of the hall emerged around our table congratulating her and each in turn giving her a hug and kiss. Then a cheeky face appeared in front of her, it was James.

He and Louise looked at each other for a moment and then he grabbed hold of her and held her tight for the first time in years whispering that he was so proud of her and loved her. Both Ryan and I were overwhelmed at this unexpected flow of emotion from him and knew at last he had forgiven her and at the same time himself for not being able to help her. We know we still have a long way to go but we are determined to carry on together as always.

The beginning.

# The Authors View About The Book

How can drug addiction be tackled? In my opinion detoxing an addict is just the start, you cannot expect a drug addict to get clean and then lead a normal life immediately. They need at least six months to be rehabilitated, with intense therapy. More understanding is needed within the community and more training for the professionals. In many cases they have started young so re-training through recovery could be an answer, to give them a purpose, and for them to realise that although it is a scary world out there, they have the ability to succeed and move forward in a positive way.

I noticed that in my experience when clean, drug users tend to create another addiction, in our case Lou was totally committed to her art. Gary has since become addicted to gardening, which we are most grateful for, so whether it be exercise, art, gardening or anything else, addiction can sometimes be put into good use. We need to understand that drug users do not like, or want, to live the life they are forced to live through their addiction.

We need to educate children about the horrors of this terrible illness. In my view the best way to tackle that is to get teachers and parents involved in making sure the correct information is available not only for the user but more importantly the parent and it is easily accessed. All schools should have an anti-drug mentor within the school, this would enable the right advice to be available to parents that may have concerns about their child. Telling them what signs to look for would be a great help, when our daughter was acting strangely we assumed it was teenage behaviour.

This might also help tackle the problem of the dealers that intimidate the vulnerable outside the schools. Get willing ex users to go to the schools and show the children what it would be like to live as an addict. This would be another good way to inform the parents to the dangers and symptoms of drug abuse. At the same time it could help the recovering addict to come to terms with his or her illness. Have help within the schools for children that have parents that are addicted. Once the parents discover that they have a real problem with drug abuse, I know from experience that there is only limited support out there, but in fairness I now understand that every case is different and that there is no template that fits all, but keeping parents in the loop with information would be a big help.

Whilst I understand that patient confidentiality is important, I think when it comes to drug addiction there should be a way of having a mentor that would work with the users key worker to keep the parents informed and help them to help their child, and if they are in a position to detox at home, they should be given the courtesy of being in more control of the situation, with the proper advice and not be isolated by the professionals, as they are already isolated by their child.

I do not have the answers and in many cases I suspect some of my suggestions are already in place but after being in contact with other parents in a similar situation I have found that the most prominent criticism is the lack information.

My son has now come to terms with the last few years events and is now building bridges with his sister. Emma is still battling to get help for Alex as he continues to have problems with drugs, but now she is not alone as she is getting married to a wonderful man that supports her and both of her sons.

Holly and Paul remain happy and are so proud of Louise for coming through her addiction. I am very grateful they were there for James when he needed it. Ryan is still wary of the fact that the reason she took drugs in the first place is still an issue, not only with Lou but with him as well, time will tell were that will go. As for me, my most surprising achievement is that

I can now do injections. This is ironic when you think about it. I understand more about the importance of being judgemental of people without knowing the facts. I have more faith in my own ability to overcome. Although at times I thought I would lose my mind, the mother instinct in me seemed to bring me back and face the next challenge. I have forgiven myself for not recognising my daughters pain and know that in the future I will still make mistakes as we all do but I accept I am only human.

This story is supposed to be a positive one, to maybe give hope to any other parent going through a terrible time, and to say although you may not have the same outcome that we have had, there is hope and with help you will succeed.

IF YOU BELIEVE YOU WILL ACHIEVE!

# Louise's Story

*It had been a real wrench to leave all my friends when we moved to our new home in the village. The education system here works differently from my previous area. After being in a middle school that had an age group of nine to thirteen year olds I was put in a primary class and I felt as if I had taken a step back.*

*It was also very hard to fit in, as my classmates had already made their friends and even my accent seemed to cause them problems. I was very self-conscious of my weight as I felt I was a bit fat.*

*When changing to my secondary school I was still feeling isolated and had not seemed to gel with my peers, although I had friends I had no-one that I could call close.*

*I was about thirteen when I started experimenting with pot as this was socially acceptable within the group that I hung around with and I wanted to fit in. I also took prescription pills from my Mums first aid box and took them with alcohol, as anything would do.*

*After I suffered from the rape, I could not trust anyone, and did not want to talk about my feelings. Although other people could see that I was changing, I was unable to open up to anyone. My teacher took me aside one day as she was worried about my change in behaviour, but it made no difference. I had become very disruptive, and because I had always been quiet and in the background, she could not understand why this was happening to me, and I could not explain to her, or anyone else, why this was happening either.*

*A few people in the year above me had started using harder drugs and I became friendly with them and they showed me where they went to get their supply. After I stopped seeing Sammi, as she had betrayed me and I could not bear to be with her anymore, I began to wander around on my own careful not to get too close to anyone. One day a young man approached me and I recognised him from school.*

*He had been expelled after I had started, and I had only seen him a couple of times as he was older than me. Although we had not really spent any time together before, he seemed friendly and we started chatting. I was dubious at first as I was frightened that he might attack me as I had lost all trust in men, but after a while felt comfortable with him and over the next few weeks, we would meet up and talk about our past and how we felt about everything.*

*Gary had been in trouble with the police as he got in with the wrong crowd and like me tried to fit in by going along with what his friends did, as it was his only escape from the life he had at home.*

*After returning from Greece I could not wait to see Gary again as he had become my only friend.*

*When I finally felt comfortable enough for him to meet Mum and Dad, he was so nervous he could not look them in the eye when he spoke to them, and I could tell Mum did not like him.*

*As time went on things got worse for me as I was having flashbacks over the attack and could not cope with the memory of it. I had from an early age learnt to keep my emotions under control and just keep in the background, I don't know why I did this but it just seemed easier that way for me,*

*My only saviour seemed to be heroin as it numbed the feelings and helped me get through each day.*

*I told Gary after a while what I was doing, he was angry with me but tried it out to understand what was so good about using it. Unfortunately it backfired and he quickly became addicted, leaving me feeling very guilty that I was the cause of his addiction.*

*Having to hold down a job whilst being an addict was difficult as I was bullied in my workplace, by a jealous co-worker, and at the same time I was trying to function well enough to do my job properly. I did not realise at the time that I was not functioning as well as I thought and started to make mistakes with my job.*

*After talking to Gary about wanting to get off the drugs he told me that it was time to tell Mum and Dad that I needed to get a detox and get better. As it was near Christmas and I had two weeks holiday leave owed to me, I decided to come clean and get the help. At the same time Gary was going to start a programme too.*

*As I was only sixteen the home Lofexideine detox was my only option.*

*I was to be monitored and counselled by the nurses which I was pleased about.*

*I felt my Mum should have also had more help as she seemed to be ignored a lot, but I wanted my treatment to be confidential as I was not ready to be honest about my addiction in front of her.*

*I felt uncomfortable and ashamed as I thought I was a bad person bringing more upset for my parents.*

*My mum thought I had a lot of support after the detox, but the truth was that the promises that both Gary and I would be detoxed at the same time did not happen because of funding not being available, so this left me vulnerable as he was still using drugs.*

*It was not long before I was back on it again.*

*Money was disappearing as soon as I earnt it so I was getting tick from the dealers.*

*I trusted the dealers when they said they would wait for the money, but ended up being threatened at my workplace, that was when I realised I would have to tell my parents again and get help.*

*After kicking up a fuss both Gary and I managed to persuade our key workers and doctor that we could go on a methadone maintenance programme, to cut out the use of heroin altogether. Later that day I had to meet Dad as he was going to pay my debt off to the dealer.*

*When we got home my parents decided that I should stay at home not see Gary and re-train for another job.*

*I had to comply as I felt I had no choice, and it made me feel like my parents were trying to control me and I felt trapped.*

*After a couple of months I needed to talk to someone and I missed Gary so much that I managed to arrange a meeting with him.*

*Over time we met on a regular basis, I did not like going behind my parents back but I wished they could see Gary for who he really was, not their perception of him.*

*The worst thing happened one morning when my parents found out I had been deceitful to them and they carried out the threat of making me homeless, as they were convinced I had lied about everything else and they had lost trust in me.*

*From that moment on I felt no-one cared and sunk deeper into my addiction again.*

*I had nowhere to live for months and ended up in a tent in someone's garden, just trying to get through each day.*

*I felt that my parents did not love me anymore and was very alone.*

*My sister saw the state I was in and told Mum and Dad, they, in their wisdom bought me a caravan so that I could be safe and near them while I got clean, but I again felt trapped as they had arranged for me to live under their supervision but not part of the family.*

*Lucky for me I was not in the caravan for too long as my keyworkers found me a temporary flat in a nearby town, so I left as soon as I could, little knowing that this would turn out to be even worse for me.*

*Gary moved in with me unbeknown to my family as they did still not like him as they were convinced he was to blame for everything, and they did not want to hear anything different.*

*My key worker had now become my main support.*

*The flats we were in was full of other drug addicts and alcoholics and as we were living amongst so many dysfunctional people, Gary and I sank deeper into our addiction, resorting to shoplifting to support our ever growing habit, and I developed a needle fixation.*

*It was about this time that Holly my sister confronted me about my behaviour, I was at my lowest ebb, resulting in my breaking down, and admitting to her that I had been raped.*

*This was very hard for me as I knew that Mum and Dad would now be told, and this I could not do, as I could not cope with having to relive it over again. Holly said she would tell them and I waited for the outcome, wondering if they would believe that I was telling the truth.*

*The next day both Mum and Dad came to see me and we spent most of the day together talking about everything. They showed me they cared and I felt that for once I was not being judged.*

*Drugs make you paranoid and can give mental illness, so it was not surprising when I look back, that I had irrational thoughts of not being loved or valued by my family, as every action by them seemed to always have a negative reaction from me.*

*For some reason that I still do not understand, I felt I had always been on the outside looking in, and while James seemed to be able to express his feelings I could not.*

*After the fire we moved back home for a while and I took this opportunity to tell my Mum about Gary and the truth about his childhood.*

*Finally I was getting through and Mum seemed to listen to me.*

*I was devastated when I found out that Grandad was going to die and I promised him I would get better, I am glad I was able to tell him this when I last saw him.*

*At the funeral both Gary and I felt we were not a party to the proceedings as my brother had refused to travel with us in the procession, so we had to go with my Dad in his car. I felt James always seemed to get his way and I wished that he would look at me and not judge, as he did not know how hard it was for me to get through each day with the memories of my rape still so vivid in my head.*

*After the funeral my Mum came to my flat and once again told me she was going to leave me and said some very hurtful things to me.*

*I felt that I was justified in thinking that she did not love me, and did not want me to be part of her life and I truly felt abandoned again.*

*Little did I know at the time this was far from the truth and that both my parents were trying their best to shock me into getting back to health again.*

*They thought the tough love approach would work and this time it may have. But it left me feeling suicidal, lucky for me Gary helped me through the next few months.*

*I was missing my family and my little cat that used to run down to the caravan and keep me company. Then as luck would have it I was given the chance to look after a rescue dog, giving me the opportunity to take responsibility for the welfare of an animal.*

*She was a sweet little terrier, both Gary and I fell in love with her and enjoyed taking her out for walks together.*

*This was to be a turning point and I began to feel ready to get my life back again.*

*As Christmas approached I got a phone call from Dad saying he was coming round and*

*I was pleased but reserved as I was worried that I would be disappointed again but I was happily wrong.*

*I rang Christmas day and spoke to Mum for the first time since our last meeting and it was a relief to be able to talk to her without feeling an outcast.*

*After Gary's detox in February, Mum and Dad seemed to warm to Gary and it made me feel more relaxed and pleased that they were beginning to see him as he really is.*

*After my final detox I started college and began to feel alive. I spent most of my time studying for my art degree as this helped with my recovery, keeping me focussed, and I had begun to get closer to my family again, so life seemed to be a lot better.*

*Little did I know that life had another surprise for me.*

*We were still feeling under the weather when after a routine blood test Gary was given the* news that he had Hepatitis c, and after I was tested I proved positive as well.

When we found out that both Gary and I had hepatitis it was like a smack in the face, after everything we had been through I felt we were being tested again.

Mum helped me as best she could by supporting me and reassuring me we would be allright.

For the first time Mum was not being shut out by me or the professionals. We were together all the time when going to all my appointments and generally she was in my corner. I was amazed she even learnt how to give me my injections. I felt that at last we were getting closer after so many years of being strangers, and for the first time I felt I was getting to know my real Mum.

After going through a radical treatment I came out the other side better physically and mentally.

*What I have learnt from all of this?*

1   I have learnt that no matter what is in store for me, I will be able to overcome as I have the support of my family.

2   I have learnt how to show my emotions more and not be afraid to be truthful about how I am feeling, as people will assume the worst if the wrong information is given.

3   I live with my addiction daily and will always have to be strong, but with my families love and support know that I will succeed

4   The most important thing I have discovered is that I know that whatever my parents did, rightly or wrongly, when I was using drugs, was out of their unconditional love for me and not through their indifference.

*Vanessa Wales was born in 1950 in the town of Bromley in Kent. She left school at the age of fifteen and started work in Hatton Garden training to be a Diamond Sorter. After a year she left to start an apprenticeship in hairdressing. She married in 1969, and had two daughters. In 1981 she opened her first salon in Erith Kent, and two years later having become a single parent went on to open another salon in Bexleyheath. After re-marrying she sold her businesses had two more children and settled down to domestic life. It was not long before she became restless, so with the help of her friend Sue they both became dolls house miniaturists, making tiny period hats for dolls houses, selling them all over the world through fairs and even supplying them to Hamleys the famous toy*

*store in London. When asked to write an article for the Dolls House World magazine, Vanessa jumped at the chance and after completing the first one, became a regular writer for the magazine. In 1997 she moved again to the west country and worked in a residential home as an activities organiser. Part of her remit was to produce a monthly newsletter for the residents, containing stories about some of their lives. She now lives in Dorset with her husband with family nearby. This is her first book.*

Lightning Source UK Ltd.
Milton Keynes UK
UKOW01f0848271016
286227UK00001B/7/P